# Organizing School Journeys

## Michael James Arkinstall

## Ward Lock Educational

43589

ISBN 0 7062 3608 4

First published 1977

Filmset in 11 on 12 point Times
and printed by Willmer Brothers Limited, Birkenhead
for Ward Lock Educational
116 Baker Street, London, W1M 2BB
Made in Great Britain

# Contents

# Acknowledgments

The author and publishers would like to thank the City of Birmingham Education Department for permission to reproduce the Stansfeld parents' and medical consent forms in Appendix 2, and Oxfordshire County Council, Department of Museum Services for permission to reproduce the worksheet *Potteries by the Roman Road* in Appendix 4.

# Preface

I have been extremely fortunate during my teaching career to meet and work with many dedicated colleagues. Although they may have disagreed about ideologies or methods they have shared one belief: in teaching, success is directly proportional to effort and determination. This theme is particularly true with regard to school trips, visits and journeys. If they are to be worthwhile they must be well planned and carried out with energy and fortitude. In this part of the curriculum there is no room for the sloppy, careless planner: omissions can easily lead to disaster.

Working in a Birmingham consortium means working together and sharing ideas unselfishly and I would like to acknowledge the advice and the contributions of many of my colleagues. They have helped to make the text of this little book meaningful by offering details of their own experiences with children, and I thank them all for their enthusiasm, especially as they responded so quickly to my call for aid.

I would like to dedicate this work to my former Head, my constant critic and my best adviser, Elwyn Jackson of Yenton Junior School, Erdington.

Michael James Arkinstall
July 1976

# Introduction

In our democratic society no one need ever suffer from lack of advice. Indeed, there are always people ready to offer a comment, a criticism or a helpful and timely word of wisdom. Inevitably, certain phrases become commonplace whilst others offer a deeper significance. 'Stand up: speak up and shut up' is sensible for those embarking on a career of public speaking. Teachers, however, are usually very good at doing the first two things and pretty hopeless in respect of the last one. It seems to be an occupational hazard that the people who are really dedicated educationalists find it extremely difficult to keep quiet. Holiday jaunts and exciting parties are often marred by the teachers' delight in talking shop whenever an opportunity presents itself. One might almost invent a new disease – 'lexicosis' – to describe the fertile and animated approach, the verbal propaganda, by which teachers discuss their views and experiences in an attempt to clarify and improve education.

The truth of the matter is that education is a powerful topic and one in which every person is involved; the trouble is that everyone also thinks they know what is best for their children. Somehow or other the professional educationalist has to mediate between the demands and pressures of society which is constantly dynamic and changing and the limited capacity of the school situation which may be both static and inert. There is often a vast gulf between what may be termed theory and practice.

But most of the current educational debate has evolved around the concept of 'curriculum', which is considered to be wide ranging and comprehensive in its scope. The school itself has tasks and duties to fulfil by formal lessons and activities, but there is an increasing awareness that education is more than just the learning of facts or knowledge. The informal aspect of the

7

curriculum goes beyond the school boundaries and out into the real world. Children need experiences which cannot be manufactured in the classroom and true learning is very often an active process which should not be confused with training or instruction.

The world has changed: yet many teachers are reluctant to abandon methods and rituals which have stood them in good stead in the past. But, hopefully, there is a growing trend towards relating curricula to the needs of modern society. This is most noticeable in the development of environmental studies and other out-of-school activities. In the last twenty years visits, journeys, excursions or expeditions – whether they be shortlived and near at hand or far ranging and exhaustive – have slowly become accepted as a regular feature of school life. This book is intended to show the value of such activities and to discuss practical issues, bearing in mind that 'actions often speak louder than words'.

Chapter 1

# A justification

**What is a school?**
At first sight this seems a stupid, worthless question for a practical book. Everybody who can read it has been to school and knows full well what a school is. But do they? Have they ever thought deeply about the subject?

In this day and age schools are changing as society in general, and parents and children in particular, expect more and more from teachers. Some critics point out that schools are not responding fast enough in the age of technology. Man can achieve tremendous scientific advances and yet some children leave school unable to read or carry on a sensible conversation. Cynics suggest that there is a vast gulf between what happens in the world outside where changes are rapid, and what goes on in schools which are subject to conservatism and inertia. They proclaim and predict a total irrelevance of school lessons unless curricula are drastically rebuilt to suit modern demands and pressures.

Very few sociologists would be brave enough to draw up a blueprint for success in schools. Perhaps that would deny the liberty of the teacher or destroy the individuality of schools. The teacher must draw what help and inspiration he can from official reports and recommendations. The Bullock Report (DES 1975) suggested that literacy itself might be a useful standard for assessment of school work but it was eager to point out that 'it is obvious that as society becomes more complex and makes higher demands in awareness and understanding of its members, the criteria of literacy will rise'. No man can absorb the growing amount of factual knowledge which is being accumulated and schools, surely, can be forgiven if they go along with the Hadow Report (Ministry of Education 1931) which spoke of the value of experiences as opposed to 'knowledge to be gained and facts to be stored'.

It is in the realm of its approach to the curriculum that the modern primary school becomes both exciting and perplexing.

**Views on the curriculum**
Difficulties arise in trying to define the concept of curriculum, but there is a growing acceptance that the term includes materials and methods as well as subjects or contents. Activities which take place out of school and beyond the normal opening hours are now considered to fall properly within the scope and realm of curriculum studies. Approaches vary considerably from school to school and place to place and, in practice, few schools can be classified as being purely 'traditional', 'progressive' or 'reconstructionalist'.

In his book on Summerhill, A. S. Neill (1968) identified himself as a modern progressive by saying, 'When my wife and I began the school we had one main idea: "to make the school fit the child – instead of making the child fit the school".' This was his particular strategy for social renewal and it is very interesting to note that lessons were optional.

A more up-to-date development is described by Henry Pluckrose (1975) in his concept of an open school for today's children: 'Our aim must surely be to enable children to enter their inheritance, to give them a sense of order in a chaotic and ever-changing world, so to structure their experiences that learning is meaningful and to enable them to have a vision of their future and preserve their ideals.' For him, school and society are inseparable: each complements the other, but school must be shaped to fit today's world outside. In such a situation there can be very little wrong with carefully planned and properly prepared visits out of school if they provide useful experiences. He quotes the example of John, aged nine, who visits Glastonbury: such an experience enriches his school life and he returns to the city keen to make further historical and geographical studies in the classroom.

**Learning from experience**
Studies of child development have stressed both the individual and the collective needs of children with the result that the emphasis has switched from teaching to learning. In the process the teacher's task has become harder rather than easier. It is relatively easy to give a lecture or a lesson to a captive audience

but it is extremely difficult to create a learning environment in an ordinary classroom which will satisfy the needs of each child in the class. No teacher can ever achieve complete success. Practical compromises may help one to achieve job satisfaction. Perhaps an increasing use of the facilities of the wider community – libraries, museums, parks and streets will compensate for the deficiencies of the classroom.

Ideologically, it is easy to see the value of going out of school. The greatest difficulty is in the realm of logistics. Who is going to take the children out? What will they do? How will they behave when released from the shackles of the school environment? If only a small group are going out, what will the others do and who will take responsibility for them? How can one justify the work outside? What are the specific objectives? So the long debate continues. Teacher inertia may sometimes lead to an exaggeration of the difficulties.

**New horizons**
Properly planned and conducted, trips out of school add a further dimension to a child's awareness and understanding of his world. On a visit to Peter Scott's Wildfowl Trust at Slimbridge there was a first-class exhibition in the entrance corridor, which many guests chose to pass with only a cursory glance. In the middle of one display the visitor looks into a mirror only to see the caption: 'Here is nature's greatest enemy: Man himself'. It's a sobering thought, but the current emphasis on pollution and conservation backs up the truth of the assertion. This reminder, just as much as the collection of wildfowl, serves to emphasize the importance of environmental studies.

The most important motive behind this 'environmental studies approach' is that children should learn about the world in which they live by first-hand observation and discovery. This includes going out of school, though not necessarily going as far as Slimbridge, London or the Hebrides. In the narrower, operational sphere it may mean going to a local farm, house or city street: in the wider sense it could mean an overnight expedition into completely new territory. School walls and fences are looked upon as artificial restraints for those who wish to use the environment as a focus for learning experiences. Moreover the school grounds themselves often have untold possibilities. The Project Environment team (Schools Council 1975) have this to say on the subject:

Sometimes work in the school grounds can be a preliminary or a follow-up or a supplement to a particular classroom activity or out of school visit. Sometimes it can offer quite different and new teaching opportunities. Our contention is that the school grounds should be so planned and maintained as to encourage every teacher, whatever his subject, to use them when he feels that this will enliven his teaching. They should become a place which positively invites such activity. All too often they are somewhere where organized games are played and which must be kept tidy, any other use being considered an encroachment on this complacent regime.

Those teachers and children who share an 'inner ring' school where never a blade of grass is to be seen can use instead an 'urban trail'. This innovation consists of a preplanned route in the vicinity of the school. The trackers, as the users are called, travel along the course and observe certain points and features of interest. Sketch pads, cameras and cassette recorders are used to preserve a record of what is seen and heard. That's one way of joining the technological revolution! Each school can create its own trail which will provide new stimuli at different seasons of the year.

Young infants can benefit from a walk out of school, purely as a spontaneous response to the weather. But how more meaningful a properly planned expedition will be – even if it starts and finishes only a stone's throw away from the classroom. The golden rule for success is that the teacher should have passed that way before. He will then be amply prepared for some of the things which might happen *en route*. Later chapters will be devoted to the questions of preparation.

Eric Midwinter (1975) made it clear that teachers have a definite responsibility to take their children out of school when he stated: 'A principal goal of the school might be the familiarization of the child with his own immediate environment – warts and all.' The environment is full of possibilities and children may be encouraged to acquire discernment and a critical faculty as they are taught to look carefully at what they see outside without wearing rose-coloured spectacles. Town trailing and using the locality has proved to be a valuable stimulus in Liverpool and New York. Handled carefully and with preparation by the teacher, short trips out of school could improve the quality and relevance of the curriculum.

## Conclusion

Trying to be realistic and practical, it is very difficult to see how any school can afford to rely entirely upon domestic and indoor experience if its work is to be relevant to the needs of society. The reluctance of the teacher to forsake his comfortable classroom domain can be overcome by demonstrating how effective properly planned and interesting work out of school can be.

Children from the author's school have established several outside links. Visits to the city's reference library to study documents of all sorts have shown teachers, parents and children the potentiality that exists for group and class projects which derive material from beyond the school boundaries.

To be successful, schools must rely on gaining help from other sectors and agencies in the wider world around them. No school can exist as an island: it must relate to the needs and pressures of the unstable society in which it is located.

Going out and about helps to extend the child's horizons. The pages which follow are an attempt to translate this statement into reality. It is quite amazing how much some teachers will do to improve the quality of schooling for their pupils.

**References**

DES (1975) *A Language for Life* (Bullock Report) HMSO

MIDWINTER, E. (1975) 'Curriculum and the EPA school' in Golby, Greenwald and West *Curriculum Design* Open University

MINISTRY OF EDUCATION (1931) *Report of the Consultative Committee on the Primary School* (Hadow Report) HMSO

NEILL, A. S. (1968) *Summerhill* Penguin

PLUCKROSE, H. (1975) *Open School, Open Society* Evans Brothers

SCHOOLS COUNCIL (1975) *School Outdoor Resource Areas* (from Project Environment 8–18) Longman

# Chapter 2

# The preparation

**How important is it?**

It is Saturday. Eight teachers from different parts of the country are taking a lunch-time drink in a bar in Manchester. The author mentions plans for a book on out-of-school activities and before he realizes what he has done, stories are being swapped with wit and spontaneity. Young Jimmy from Cheshire features in one about an anti-litter excursion to the Welsh light railway; Sam and Jonathan are heroes of a fossil-hunting team that nearly disappeared over a cliff; the anonymous description is given of 'Sir' who got lost whilst searching for a child in Westminster Abbey; the coach driver who ended up in Leek whilst looking for Jodrell Bank; the saga of the green ice lollies at Runnymede; the near disaster of a one-day trip that took Birmingham children by hovercraft to France and the unrepeatable chaos and discomfort that was experienced in an aeroplane excursion over Merseyside: all the tales would hold the interest of modern pilgrims to Canterbury. They caused great amusement in retrospect but, at the time, brought despair, fright, even agony and heartache to the teachers in charge.

Such anecdotes serve to underline the point that school trips and visits, of whatever size and importance, must be properly arranged. The human element is so strong in a group of lively youngsters that every possible precaution must be taken to ensure that nothing goes wrong which could have been avoided by careful preparation. With a strong framework of order and foreknowledge the teacher is better armed to deal with the unexpected when it arrives and every hour of preparation is time well spent. It may be looked upon as being directly proportional to the success of the expedition.

But where does the teacher start? It's all right for the 'old stagers' to criticize; they've seen it all before. But what comes first and how does one identify the priorities? There is no short answer, for every trip is a unique occasion shared by the particular group of people involved and, even if they wouldn't admit it, the experienced trip organizers find that there are certain difficulties to be overcome each time they start to plan an activity. There are, however, certain areas in which advice may be given. Very briefly, these could be classified as decision making, logistics and public relations.

**Decision making**
Few educationalists would dispute that interest is one of the greatest motivational forces, and the desire to go on many outings will be derived from the need to investigate or to experience something new. Thus many of the decisions to go out will be made as a way of enriching or introducing a topic which is being studied within the classroom. The fact that a visit is relevant is very often seen by the teacher as the justification for arranging it. But on other occasions a trip or visit may be arranged as an experience in itself, without any ulterior motive. The strange thing is that such an experience will, of itself, evoke interest in new ideas or topics and so the whole process is really self-perpetuating. The teacher's role as a decision maker is to mediate between the many and conflicting 'interest demands' and choose what is considered to be the most appropriate destination bearing in mind such factors as the age of the children, the time involved in travelling, the costs and the staffing difficulties at any given time of the year.

There is a booklet issued by the National Association for Environmental Education (1975) which goes into the details of organizing a school visit. Aims and objectives are made explicit and visits are categorized into three types:

1  going out as a stimulus to work in all aspects of the curriculum
2  a visit with a limited purpose as either (a) a starting point or (b) the confirmation of previous classwork
3  a structured visit with a specific purpose.

Whatever his choice, the teacher is given practical guidelines to help him avoid making mistakes in planning and organizing his visit. It is important to stress that the choice must be a positive and conscientious one. Frivolous or half-hearted decisions are doomed to failure! In the case of out-of-door visits and excursions half a loaf is not better than no bread.

Once the decision to go 'somewhere' and to do 'something' has been made, the real work of planning can begin in earnest. For the sake of convenience, this stage may be referred to as the exploration of logistics.

**Logistics**

For those who like definitions, logistics may be described as the study of the available resources, including time and space. There is something of the 'chicken or the egg' controversy here, for the decision to go somewhere is almost inevitably tied up with the factors which make up reality. A junior school teacher might be interested in the Eskimos, or in nuclear power stations – his children could quite conceivably be doing a project which included such topics – but never in his wildest dreams would he expect that visits to such places might be feasible. Conversely, a local project on the Civil War might lead to a visit to a stately home, or a study of wild flowers might be stimulated by a walk in the countryside: the commonsense aspect of decision making depends to a large extent on practical considerations.

Certain subdivisions might be helpful to those who are contemplating a visit and feel they need a sort of checklist – a passport to success. In their preparation they can decide upon the following points:

1  What is the purpose of the journey? Which of the three types mentioned above best describes your expectations for it? This must be decided as a matter of priority, for the remainder of the planning will be geared towards the achievement of your particular objectives. If your intention is to go out as a stimulus to work, then it will be necessary to anticipate points of interest and the particular pieces of equipment that will be needed. For example, if it is to be an urban study of a shopping centre one will need clipboards, questionnaires, cameras and possibly tape recorders.

   If it is to be an orienteering expedition, compass, maps, survival kits, first-aid equipment and contingency plans in case of emergency will be essential. In such a case, suitable clothing will be of vital importance.

   There will need to be discussions before the exercise and,

possibly, preparatory work in the classroom. Map reading does not come naturally and children need training in how to interview passers-by! It will be necessary to consider if the visit will have to be reinforced with follow-up work. This is a vital point, for there should be some record of the visit, be it on slide, tape or paper.

2 How long will the journey or visit last? Is it half a day, a full day, several days, or even a week or more? Generally speaking, the longer the visit, the more preparation will be required. If the journey means that the children have to stay overnight or for several nights then the whole dimension of the planning changes, though a longer stay at one place need not necessarily be a great deal harder to plan than an itinerary which takes in several different stopping places. So a trip to the reference library to look at documents might mean only a few phone calls and a letter to parents, whilst a cruise to Corunna might entail almost a military campaign which is very carefully enacted by chapter and verse. Travelling abroad should really be considered separately, for it imposes a whole new range of limitations and possibilities.

3 Staffing ratios are usually laid down by local authorities. These depend to a great extent upon the nature of the expedition and its scope. The teacher will have to check on these locally. Some authorities have the norm of one teacher to twenty pupils, but this can be unsatisfactory in all but the most mundane activities. The staff must also be sympathetic and healthy. A teacher who can't bear the cold and hates to miss his colour television will be no use on a camping expedition to central Wales. If there is to be a mixed group then there will have to be both male and female staff present in spite of what any 'liberated' people might suggest.

4 Transport arrangements can be a real constraint on intentions. If the trip entails travelling a long distance, then the relative merits of coach or train, ship or plane will have to be considered. One of the worst hazards with children is sickness. This is particularly difficult to overcome when travelling by coach on a hot summer's day. Sickness pills, sand buckets, polythene bags or sitting on a piece of newspaper all help, as do the many and varied folk remedies, but the teacher must be ready to cope if the 'dreaded lurgi' strikes. Coaches have two advantages: to begin with they can travel from door to door (there's no running down the tube or

B

racing from one platform to the other with heavy luggage); they also keep the party together, under the eagle eye of the teacher. But against this one must weigh the advantages of travelling on a corridor train with toilet and buffet facilities. Such a comparison could be made and costed for, say, a trip from Birmingham to London, but in practice there may be only one suitable arrangement for the particular plans the reader has in mind.

If there is only a small group, then car or minibus might be the answer, though the insurance and costs of such excursions should be carefully and comprehensively explored. More will be said about that under the heading of responsibility. On field study courses it is often essential to have some means of transport 'on site', if only to deal with emergencies; though such a facility can greatly increase the scope and efficiency of the mission.

5    Tied in with choice of transport is the financial aspect. The more adventurous the trip and the more people who are involved, the greater the global commitment; though it should be remembered that the economies of scale operate as well as the law of diminishing returns. It is a moral issue as to whether children should subsidize their peers or whether children should miss opportunities because their parents can't afford to pay. There must somewhere be a balance between encouraging scroungers and helping those in genuine need. Once again some education authorities will help with grants when there is insufficient money in the kitty. It is interesting to note here that sponsorship has grown apace in recent years. At least two of the twenty-six chess teams involved in the most recent Inter-Association Chess Tournament for Primary Schools' Children raised money for their expenses by means of a sponsored chess display. Some teachers would claim that, with regard to money, where there's a will there's a way: others might think it beneath their professional dignity to help to raise funds. But most would agree that it's a pity if little Willy misses out through no fault of his own.


It is almost impossible to categorize that precious quality of enthusiasm – the person who organizes the school trip will need plenty of that commodity when he starts to consider the realm of logistics.

## Public relations

In considering the public relations aspect of trips, tours and visits, one is moving into the complex realm of sociology.

Society at large is concerned at many levels with children 'out of school'. If one can assume that any given excursion is a success in the terms of the organizer's criteria, there is still the consideration of how the event affected other people. Were the children polite? Did they leave litter? Could they go back again and be well received? Have they shared their good fortune with others by telling them or showing them what happened? Was the visit purposeful and have they gained from it? Have they thanked their hosts? These are just some of the questions which spring instantly to mind when one starts to think of the wider implications.

It is easy to forget the parents, as many innovators have found to their cost. But, as the Plowden Report (DES 1967) emphasizes, they can be a real support and a great ally to the teacher who is dedicated to improving the quality of the child's education:

> There is certainly an association between parental encouragement and educational performance. This does not tell us which way round the relationship is. Is performance better where parents encourage more? Do parents encourage more where performance is better? Common sense suggests that each factor is related to the other, and both are related to the work of the school itself. Homes and schools interact continuously. An improvement in school may raise the level of parental interest and that, in its turn, may lead to further improvement in school – or deterioration may also be cumulative . . .
>
> Schools exist to foster virtuous circles. They do this most obviously through their direct influence upon children. Where teachers help children to grow intellectually and emotionally, their very success is likely to evoke a response from the parents.

Similarly, where boredom and failure are constant companions there is likely to be an even stronger response!

In planning a trip the parents must be consulted. In most cases their approval and permission will be a basic requirement. This can only be achieved by the reciprocal processes of communication and cooperation. It is therefore necessary to draw up a written outline of the visit or trip and pass this on to the parents. Detailed information should be given whenever it is possible. An example of this is shown below, where a recent letter is reproduced. The actual letter was given out to all the children selected to play in a very important chess match and below the information was a tear-off slip for the parents to sign, giving their permission.

Dear Colleague,

The following player from your school has been selected to represent Birmingham in the National Inter-Association Team Championship in Manchester on Saturday, 1 May 1976:

The cost to the player will be £1.00. On this occasion we are going to travel by train, so please note the following arrangements:

9.55 am   Train departs from New Street Station. All members of the team should assemble in the station concourse by 9.30 am. You will appreciate that it is not possible to wait for anyone after that time, as we have to take our place on the train. The actual championship is being held at the Manchester College of Commerce, Aytoun Street, near Piccadilly Station. A cooked lunch and, later, an apple and chocolate for the return journey will be provided.

6.28 pm   Train departs from Manchester Piccadilly for the return journey.

8.10 pm   The expected time of arrival at New Street.

The consent form below must be completed by parents and returned to me on or before Thursday, 29 April.

Yours sincerely

David Johnson (Secretary)

The letter is brief, simple and to the point. There is no need to refer to chess problems – the children know all about playing the game. But the parents will know where they are going, how they will get there and what time they can be expected home.

Behind the letter – something the parents and children will

never normally hear about – have been the chess committee's discussions and decisions. All the logistics have been gone into – it has been planned as a military maneuvre. In this case train is considered better than coach: it is cheaper; the players will be rested and will not be travel-sick when they play that first important game. The venue is within walking distance of the station and there are no awkward obstacles to overcome like changing trains or depending upon someone else to be on time to meet the party at its destination.

The behaviour and the performance of the chess players on this particular occasion proved that the effort spent was worthwhile and the children were worthy ambassadors of their schools and their city. It also emphasized the dedication of the teachers who accompanied them.

**Communication**
One of the most overworked words, communication, covers the vital preparatory act of making sure everyone concerned knows what is happening and when and where it will take place.

In its *Notes for Guidance* one West Midlands authority puts it quite succinctly under certain headings:

1   WHO – will be able to go on the visit; will escort the party; may accompany the party from outside the school; is the principal organizer
2   WHAT – activities the party will be undertaking and under what conditions
3   WHERE – the party will be going; it will be accommodated (address and type of accommodation)
4   WHEN – the party will leave Birmingham; the party will return to Birmingham
5   HOW – the party will travel; much the visit will cost; payments are to be made.

The party leader should have with him a list of details such as the names and addresses of the party members and their phone numbers. It is wise to have an arrangement with 'someone back at the ranch' in case of emergencies and even if telephone calls are to be actively discouraged (they can cause homesickness, and this can spread like wildfire) there should be some prearranged way in which teachers and parents can communicate with each other. Such a portfolio should also include any particular medical details and consent forms which may be necessary when children are separated from their parents by time and distance. But more about that later.

There is nothing more embarrassing for a headteacher than to be asked by a parent where his child is or what time the children will be back at school when, by an oversight, the teacher has failed to give him the details. It is wise to err on the side of caution and specify every last piece of information. This can only lead to efficiency and a good image.

**A recipe for success**

If the preparations are well done, predictable disasters will be avoided, and even if the trip is not an overwhelming success it won't be a complete failure. The NAEE booklet already mentioned offers a checklist which is almost a 'top twenty' to a successful visit:

1   Take responsibility for the children at all times. [The old stager might define this as 'count them every three minutes'.]
2   Give the class a number of briefing sessions prior to the visit. Make sure that the class is fully acquainted with the organization of the visit and the rules and regulations. [Some teachers sit the children in their 'trip seats' the day before and practise their groupings during a 'dry run'.]
3   Suggest to parents that children who are prone to travel sickness take a travel sickness pill before they start out for school. Sit children prone to travel sickness near the front and have materials to deal with nausea with you (bucket, newspapers, polythene bags). Children who are taken ill may need appropriate medical attention. Too much should not be made of this in front of the children or suggestion may result in the whole group succumbing.
4   Take care in boarding coaches and trains. This must be done in an orderly queue.
5   Make the children sit in their seats during the journey. Moving about a coach is dangerous and one cause of travel sickness.
6   Have occupations for the journey. If the return journey is long it is often desirable to organize games, singing, quizzes.
7   Packed meals should be eaten only at meal times. It is not advisable to take bottled fizzy drinks.

8   When visiting places of interest, it is best to split the class into groups with a member of staff in charge of each group.
9   Make frequent checks of numbers within the class and groups, for example before entering and after leaving any places of interest. [Don't bring an extra one back.]
10  Make frequent checks of equipment, especially if engaged in fieldwork. [Don't leave your own camera on the coach-rack.]
11  When escorting the children outside, always have responsible adults to lead and to supervise the rear of the party, with an agreed procedure for crossing roads.
12  Ensure that children can be observed by an adult member at all times. [This may be difficult when it comes to toilets!]
13  Make frequent stops at toilets. [Try to locate these on preliminary visit.]
14  On long visits allow for periods of recreation. [Watch that football!]
15  Have a regard for the behaviour of the class. Aim for a high standard of behaviour at all times. If there is a lack of discipline the visit will be a disaster and a disgrace – there are many who criticize such matters as litter, noise and manners. [Here's the public relations again.]
16  Make sure that the children thank their hosts for the visit.
17  If the return is later than anticipated it is the teacher's responsibility to see that the children get home safely.
18  An identification card or disc with details to cover emergencies is useful.
19  A suitable first-aid kit is needed.

**The sixth sense**
A great deal of this chapter sounds like common sense and some of the topics mentioned will be dealt with elsewhere. The best way to see how the theory works out is to read an account, prepared in retrospect, of a successful trip where patience, preparation, humour and tolerance combined with a zest for adventure. The approach of Doreen Gower (former Deputy of Lyndhurst School) is a recipe for a successful journey:

'A school trip should not be just an outing for pure enjoyment. It should be a learning experience linked to classroom work. The trip should either spark off work in the classroom; be the culmination of such work; or bridge a gap between one project and another.

'Our project had been based upon Tudors and Stuarts: it was an historical theme. We had considered houses, costumes and, of course, the Gunpowder Plot. So our trip was planned with this in mind. We had also considered conservation and felt that "Birdland" at Bourton-on-the-Water would provide the opportunity and give that essential part of every school trip – enjoyment.

'How could a trip be planned to cover all the aspects we wanted in nine or ten hours? This is a problem of preparation and it is vitally important for anyone contemplating a trip to have visited the places on the itinerary themselves beforehand. All the details and timings should then be worked out so that the day itself will go smoothly.

'As it happened on this particular day we also had a partial eclipse of the sun – something which had not been bargained for when the first tentative arrangements were made. We left school at 8.15 and made for Coughton Court. This was chosen not only for the age and beauty of the actual building but also because the wives of the conspirators in the Gunpowder Plot waited there for their husbands to return and the coats of arms of the families concerned are set in one of the stained glass windows. Another thing of interest at Coughton was the "one day coat". Sheep were sheared early in the morning, the wool was cleaned, carded, spun, woven and dyed. From the resulting material a coat was cut and the master would wear it the same evening. The house also contained some superb ceilings and some most attractive woodwork. The grounds are beautiful and there was an avenue of lovely trees. Unfortunately some of these natural features have been spoiled by recent developments and the need to cut down certain trees. Coughton is also famous for the breeding of Pekes but we didn't see any on this occasion.

'So we left Coughton and drove through beautiful country to Birdland at Bourton-on-the-Water. This is a fascinating place where the colourful macaws fly freely about, nest in barrels or come down to hold conversations with the many visitors. Most of the children found the penguins the high spot and we had the greatest difficulty in persuading them to look at the other inhabitants of Birdland. At the time that we were there a new tropical house had just opened; but we did not intend to go in as the fee for admission had not been included in our budget because of the uncertainty about its actual opening date. The owner spoke to the children and asked them about likes and dislikes. When he found the trip did not include the tropical house and why, he offered us free admission. His reason? The children were so beautifully behaved that he would be pleased to let them see the new glories without extra charge. So in we went – into a steamy jungle of colourful plants, humming birds, insects and snakes.

'After leaving Birdland, somewhat regretfully, we sat by the river to eat our sandwiches and ice lollies because we needed to sustain ourselves for the next part of the trip. When the food had been eaten and the litter had been properly disposed of we went round the model village and then visited the Witchcraft Museum (now gone). Needless to say, most of the party were fascinated by the life-size nude women models displayed in connection with fertility rites: but, thanks to the experience of previous visitors, the staff were well primed to deal with, or skilfully evade, any really awkward questions and the children's attentions were drawn to "wing of bat, leg of frog, tongue of lizard etc." Anyone visiting Bourton nowadays does not have to face this hazard – the model railway has replaced the witchcraft exhibition.

'Leaving Bourton, we passed through Broadway and eventually reached our last place of interest, Harvington Hall at Chaddesley Corbett, near to Kidderminster. This is a beautiful tudor house surrounded by a moat and it really appealed to the children because of the number of secret hiding places – the hottest one by the side of the oven; the coldest right up in the roof and the largest behind some panelling in the library. It was into this last mentioned one that the children were allowed to go – ten at a time. The staff nobly resisted the temptation to sort out the menaces and leave them behind in one of these hiding places and we all gathered together for a lovely tea before starting our homeward journey. We reached school just after six o'clock. The weather was glorious and we had had a wonderful time, though we were left exhausted by the end of it all. However we felt that we would do it again because it had been such good fun.'

The changes in the details of a trip don't matter so much as the attitude and approach of the staff who arrange it and see it through to the end!

**References**
DES (1967) *Children and their Primary Schools* (Plowden Report) HMSO

NATIONAL ASSOCIATION FOR ENVIRONMENTAL EDUCATION (1975) *Organization of an Out of School Visit* NAEE Practical Guide 2, available from National Association for Environmental Education, Publications Department, Room 206, 102 Edmund Street, Birmingham 3

Chapter 3

# Responsibility

## Child and teacher

Chapter two of the Plowden Report (DES 1967) begins with the well-known words: 'At the heart of the educational process lies the child. No advances in policy, no acquisitions of new equipment have their desired effect unless they are in harmony with the nature of the child, unless they are fundamentally acceptable to him.'

But in accepting the need for a knowledge of child development as a prerequisite for successful learning one should never forget the importance of the role of the teacher. It is the teacher who is responsible for the quality of the child's education and that responsibility is not something which is shouldered lightly. Most teachers work out their careers with dedication and enthusiasm and it is only in moments of stress that the full realization of their personal responsibility is brought home to them. The law expresses it succinctly with the phrase *in loco parentis*, and the case study of a trip to a Welsh holiday resort supplies adequate illustration of the reality. When disaster strikes, the party leader or the teacher in charge knows the meaning of the American cry 'the buck stops here'. Action has to be taken and there is little chance for discussion or excuses and certainly no place for the faint-hearted. A weak and ineffective teacher could be worse than useless on an out-of-school excursion. It is wise to plan the staffing ratio for a trip so that the people going are those who get on well together. They will need confidence in each other and the ability to exercise initiative when things do not go exactly as planned. Mother Nature may supply strength in moments of trial, decisions may be made to cope with unforeseen circumstances, but that extra one adult in the party could help in 'carrying the day'. Suppose a child is injured and has to go to hospital; the other thirty children can't go along with him for the ride. The trip must continue as planned – otherwise one tragedy could be replaced by thirty and irate parents are hardly likely to be subdued, however sympathetic they may be, by hearing that little Billy's fate led to their own child's downfall. At the risk of 'looking on the black side' it is wise to consider an out-of-school activity in the light of what could happen, and careful planning will help to cover most of the eventualities.

If it is any consolation, there is *always* the unpredictable and children have a way of finding it. What does a teacher do when she discovers that an infant has a baby penguin in a duffle bag and they are half-way back from their annual visit to the zoo? Worse still, the mind boggles at the thought of trying to find one little boy in a Wembley football crowd during a schoolboys' international. Who says labels, nametapes or identity discs aren't important?

But the law demands that teachers take certain sensible precautions. It does not expect perfection, but it punishes sloppiness and inefficiency. The writer G. R. Barrell gives chapter and verse on this in his book *Teachers and the Law* (1975). If children are to be adequately cared for, then some of the rights of the parents must, if only temporarily, be transferred to the teacher:

> In other words the schoolmaster is said, to that extent, to be *in loco parentis*. He may chastise the child; if he does so unreasonably he is accountable to the law. He must take care of the child, and if he fails to do so reasonably he is accountable to the law. As Mr Justice Cave put it, 'What is the duty of the schoolmaster?' 'The duty of the schoolmaster is to take such care of his boys as a careful father would take of his boys.'

The teacher must always treat the children in his care as he would his own children. Erring on the side of caution need not result in a military regime, and a good relationship between teacher and child will be the basis for controlled yet imaginative expeditions. On the question of freedom there are no hard and fast rules. Once again it depends upon the children and the teacher. Some children could be trusted anywhere; others are a complete liability. The writer Gerald Haigh discussed this point in his book *Out of School Activities* (1974) when he said:

A lot depends, of course, on the age of the children. In the case of a stop at a motorway service station, for instance, a junior school party leader would probably want to escort the children across the car park and try to keep them in view most of the time. With fourteen-year olds, on the other hand, it might be more usual to say 'Back in fifteen minutes. Mind the traffic on the car park, and watch the prices.'

On a trip to London, I once allowed a party of thirteen- and fourteen-year olds to go off unsupervised for about two hours. I had written permission from their parents to do this, and I gave them each a sketch map and a duplicated list of hints, warnings and information about things to look at. With these children, and being in London, I think I was at the borderline of the amount of freedom which is allowable. Indeed some colleagues disagreed with me, although a teacher of my acquaintance once let a party loose in the Casbah in Tangiers.

The point to remember is that greater or lesser distance need not necessarily mean increasing or diminishing responsibility. The teacher is just as much responsible for the children in his care when they are crossing the local High Street on their way to the swimming baths as he would be when they were making the descent from Cader Idris. It is, therefore, a wise move to train the children in what is required so that a sense of routine order can be established. There should be a way of crossing roads, a procedure for entering the swimming pool or an accepted agreement of where people will sit on a coach or minibus. When these basic requirements are met the teacher will find the weight of responsibility so much easier to bear. The teacher who is in charge will demand certain forms of behaviour from the children who are in his care. If they will not cooperate it will be necessary for him to take steps to remove them from the danger zone and this may mean dropping them from a team or making them miss an opportunity. Most children will accept the teacher's rule of law when they know it is designed for their protection as well as the teacher's sanity. It is a fact of life that someone always has to be the boss and children will respect a firm teacher provided that he is consistent and fair. The teacher's main difficulty is that he will be called upon to make instant decisions as to what actions are acceptable at any given moment: without warning, he will have to weigh up a situation and decide how much freedom is to be given or what restrictions are to be imposed. Always, the prime concern will be the welfare of the children in his care and he will often be the sole arbiter – the power of the teacher, for good or evil, is unique.

## Legal pitfalls

One education authority in the West Midlands produced a collection of rules and regulations to assist heads and teachers in the fulfilment of their legal responsibilities. Under the heading of school visits and work done out of school they suggested that there should be a staffing ratio of not less than one teacher to forty pupils for local visits. A distance of ten miles from school would be the criterion. This was probably a device to make short and spontaneous missions a regular feature in the curriculum. But it is rather dangerous if it implies that it doesn't matter so much if children are not as highly supervised near to school as they will be when they are further afield. But every teacher should make it his business to find out details of the regulations in force in his authority. Ignorance of the law is no excuse for breaking it!

One teacher once claimed that the four qualities needed in a successful schoolmaster were patience, tolerance, a sense of humour and a taste for best bitter – but not, necessarily, in that order! In planning a visit one might also add wisdom – not the sort which equates with an inherent high IQ but that which is born from experience and care. The world in which we live is a materialistic one and a teacher's pay, if adequate, is certainly not excessive. A successful lawsuit could be the ruination of a teacher's financial position. For this reason alone, it seems sensible to insure a party, if only to be on the safe side. A comprehensive insurance policy without any small print 'ifs and buts' could be that hidden reserve which brings confidence and reassurance to the teacher. It might also be well received by the parents. Insurance companies issue indemnity for accidents, loss of limbs and personal injuries for a very small sum of money and this could be included in the *pro rata* cost of an excursion or, if preferred, paid for directly out of school funds. This delicate topic is written about in greater detail in chapter 7, for a wider range of possibilities and problems might then apply.

Schools operate different policies in their arrangements for out-of-school trips. In some schools the secretary does the 'donkey work': in others it is left to the individual teacher or leader. But it is important that there should be a strong and effective communications network. It can be most upsetting if one teacher finds his or her plans for an activity ruined because another teacher has planned a trip for the same children for a different activity on the same day. This problem is particularly rife in small schools where there aren't many children anyway. It is a good idea to have a large chart pinned up in the staffroom where everyone can insert details of what has been planned and on which day it will take place. In the area of responsibility teachers should not forget that they have a duty to cooperate with their colleagues as well as with children and parents. It could be disastrous if those 'back at the ranch' didn't know what was happening and when. Details should be publicized clearly, even at the risk of making the summary seem obvious and too elementary for words.

'Money is dynamite' – this could be another golden rule. If there is the slightest suspicion that 'Sir' or 'Miss' has misappropriated, borrowed or stolen any of the funds then there will be a furore. So it is important to stress that each trip which costs the parents anything should be completed with a balance sheet. It's better to be safe than sorry. One head used to insist that his staff added a small surcharge to their calculated amount to cover emergencies and unforeseen expenses. This may be considered morally wrong and yet, in these days of inflation, it may be wise to err on the side of asking for more and paying it back later if a profit is made. With fluctuations in exchange rates, trips to foreign countries are almost certain to be bedevilled by this financial uncertainty. If a large and costly expedition is planned – say, a fortnight's standing camp in mid Wales, then it is useful to open a special bank account to deal efficiently with all the moneys and transactions which will be involved.

The Birmingham Education Committee offers the following advice in its *Notes for Guidance*:

Heads are strongly recommended:
1   to keep a cash book to record all payments and receipts
2   to operate a separate bank account, preferably in joint names into which income should be paid intact
3   to obtain vouchers or receipts wherever possible in support of payments
4   to set up a system to record contributions from all participants and to issue authorized receipts to those members of staff, etc., who collect cash from pupils

5   to arrange for independent auditors (who might well
    include a parent)
6   to prepare at the conclusion of the journey a
    summarized statement of income and expenditures for
    audit examination; after such examination copies of the
    certified statement should be available for the
    information of parents whose children went on the
    journey.

The implications of item 6 are enough to bring home to any teacher the extent of his financial responsibility.

It is customary to ask parents' permission for organized trips out of school. This is usually done by sending out a duplicated sheet with details of the proposed trip and a tear-off *pro forma* which the parents sign to give their permission. The slip is really a form of indemnity, although by signing this the parent does not give up his or her rights under common law. Copies of such letters are to be found in the Appendices (pages 141–2). On rare occasions a particular parent may withhold permission and it would be very hard to justify taking that child out of school, albeit for his own benefit, in direct contravention of the parent's wishes. Luckily, in practice, most parents seek the best for their children and are only too happy to cooperate once they have confidence and faith in the school and the teacher. Successful school trips widen the horizons of the children; they also help to inculcate good public relations between school, home and society.

**Medical advice**
This section has been put together by a very experienced doctor whose delightful children were once pupils of the author. Most teachers have some medical knowledge, but the summary which follows contains sound practical advice which all 'trippers' should read.

Most teachers will respond well when faced with an emergency. The everyday care of large numbers of children must resolve itself into a whole series of minor emergencies and the special circumstances of a school trip or journey merely bring additional problems. I would venture to suggest that of these problems those associated with disease and injury give rise to the greatest degree of apprehension.

There are those cheerful optimists who regard all children as impervious to injury and disease. On the other hand the quaking pessimist expects at least one fatal accident and an outbreak of plague before the coach has actually left the school grounds. The truth lies somewhere between these two extremes and is, fortunately, much nearer to the optimistic end of the spectrum.

The following paragraphs are not intended as a 'do it yourself' guide to surgery on the M1. They are, instead, merely a collection of suggestions. Some are of a general nature, others more specific: some may cause mild controversy but I hope that all will prove useful. In general, children are a fairly healthy lot and are remarkably resistant to physical damage. The innumerable minor illnesses which prevent their attendance at school are surprisingly absent when a holiday is involved. If something does go wrong then one may take comfort from certain facts:

1  The majority of illnesses in children cause no lasting harm and will get better even if nothing is done.
2  If treatment is required then the simplest remedies will usually suffice.
3  In the British Isles and in those foreign countries likely to be visited on a school trip, medical aid is easily and quickly available.
4  Sudden death in the party is far more likely to occur in an overweight, harassed teacher than in one of his charges. The degree of reassurance obtained from this last point is in inverse proportion to the age and weight of the teacher concerned.

But now to practicalities. If possible, at least one of the accompanying adults should have attended the course of first aid lectures organized by the St John Ambulance Brigade or the British Red Cross Society. Ideally, he or she should hold a first aid certificate. In any case, the handbook of first aid, which is common to both organizations, will provide an invaluable reference book and will help to keep the panic at bay. A certain amount of panic is inevitable but an effort should be made not to show it. It is at least as important to appear to know what you are doing as actually to know!

Some problems may be anticipated and steps taken to minimize or avoid them before setting out. This applies to the known recurrent conditions and allergies such as travel sickness, hay fever, asthma and migraine. It is now almost universal practice to send parents a form explaining a forthcoming trip and to ask

c

them to indicate their acceptance of the conditions on behalf of their child. This should have space for the parents to record any recurrent illness or allergy which may arise in a particular child. It should be directly suggested that such children carry with them any necessary treatment with full instructions for its administration.

There are some illnesses which effectively prevent a child going away without a form of medical supervision. Fortunately they are usually catered for by specialist societies with particular knowledge and expertise. It may seem very kind to allow a child with some medical condition to go on a normal trip but it could prove to be an act of considerable folly and have tragic results.

MINOR INJURIES

*Bruises*
When there is no break in the skin these really need no treatment. No power on earth will 'bring out the bruise' in spite of popular belief to the contrary. A dressing, however, is always a great comfort, especially to the very young, and should be applied for this effect if no other.

*Cuts and abrasions*
When the skin is broken these are best dealt with by cleaning with disinfectant (not one which produces more pain than the injury) and the application of a dry dressing – preferably sterile. Sticking plaster should be avoided except to anchor dressings. This is because all plasters exclude air (and this includes those which are not supposed to) and the covered area rapidly becomes moist and infected. Ideal dressings are Melolin and Micropore tape. These are proprietary preparations and sold under those names. Melolin is used with its plastic film side next to the skin and does not stick even in the presence of blood. The tape can be torn with the fingers, does not cause plaster rashes, is easily removed and does let in the air. At this point I had better firmly deny any connection with or any shares in the firm concerned. There are many excellent disinfectants but probably the best at present for all purposes is Belodeine, a non-staining and non-stinging iodine solution. Dettol and Hibitone are also satisfactory. In all deep and dirty wounds the question of tetanus or lock-jaw prevention must be considered. Most children will have been vaccinated actively as babies. If this is so then a booster administered within a couple of days of the injury should be all that is required. Both at

34

home and abroad the advice of a local casualty department should be sought if in doubt.

A special type of wound in this category is a dog bite. Rabies is endemic on the continent of Europe and local advice must always be sought. In England, at least at the time of writing, this particular danger does not exist but the usual problem of tetanus does apply.

*Twists and sprains*

These need a supporting bandage of the crepe type or one of the excellent tubular elastic bandages which can be obtained in various diameters and cut to any length. They are pulled on like gloves or stockings and give good support but must be removed during sleep when the limbs are not active. Here again, the comforting effect of a dressing is well demonstrated.

*Burns and scalds*

Cold water or cold milk from a sterile bottle applied at once gives a lot of relief and minimizes the damage. Hands and feet can literally be dipped into a bowl and larger areas covered in gauze soaked in water or milk. This is used in the first minutes after a burn or scald and then a sterile dressing is applied. No creams, ointments, powders or anything else should be used. They obscure the burn and make assessment difficult and can be almost impossible to remove if hospital treatment is needed. Dry dressing may adhere to the burnt area so Vaseline gauze in a single layer is just about acceptable. Melolin is ideal. Most burns, other than very minor ones, will require some sort of hospital treatment. This may be limited to adequate and frequent change of dressings but this is in itself important. Prevention of infection is the cornerstone of burn management.

A special type of burn is sunburn. Here, as in most things, prevention is better than cure, but sunburn can be very insidious. Exposure for as short a time as thirty minutes can cause severe burns. Cold is no protection and it is the ultra-violet content of the light which does the damage and burns can occur in sub-zero temperatures. The worst symptoms develop some hours after exposure and then there is evidence to suggest that the antihistamine group of drugs (usually used for hay fever and other allergies), if given some time after exposure, will minimize the degree of burning. It is always problematical to advise the unqualified to administer drugs but it seems to me that if a child has been inadvertently and severely exposed then anything which

35

will minimize a possible serious reaction should be used. Someone in the party may have one of the group of drugs, but I will have more to say on the point later. Severe sunburn should be treated seriously and medical advice sought.

## Insect bites

There are many different types according to the locality. In the British Isles the commonest are bees and wasps, with hornets and horse flies less common. All can cause local pain and swelling but very rarely anything more serious. The fortunately rare anaphylactic reaction which can cause death in hypersensitive individuals needs urgent medical treatment and there is little one can do unless the appropriate drugs and other equipment are immediately available. Any child with known allergies should be considered especially at risk and bites treated more seriously than in others. Bites on the mouth and throat area should also be taken seriously since here simple swelling can block the breathing passages. I would stress again, however, that with very rare exceptions, insect bites are painful but harmless. Antihistamines locally and by mouth are of value in reducing the reaction. Foreign countries may boast more exotic varieties than the British Isles but the effects are unlikely to be any worse.

## Snake bites

The only indigenous poisonous snake is the viper or adder. Its bite is seldom dangerous and the most useful thing one can do is to prevent the overenthusiastic lay surgeon from attempting to incise the bite and suck out the poison. This only works in films and is quite futile in real life. Simply assure the victim that he is not going to die and get him to hospital. Do not expect the staff to meet you on the doorstep with anti-serum at the ready – it is probably at least as dangerous as the snake venom. Snake bites abroad can be serious and the nearest hospital should be contacted immediately. Here, the risks of anti-serum are far outweighed by the danger of the bite and stocks against all the local varieties of snake are kept and can be life-saving.

### EPILEPSY

A child who is known to be epileptic probably will not go on a normal school trip unless he is well controlled by drugs and unlikely to have a fit. However, a child could have his first fit on a trip. Treatment should be limited to preventing injury if there is much movement. This is accomplished by deflection rather than restraint of the arms and legs. The tongue is in danger of being bitten and so are the untrained fingers which attempt to prevent it. A pencil, or a similar wooden object, placed between the back teeth on one side is all that should be done. Medical advice is then necessary but heroic dashes to hospital with the child still fitting are out. A fit may be alarming but, left alone, the child will pass into a quiet sleep and can then be moved.

BLEEDING AND RESUSCITATION
Under these headings come some rather alarming conditions, but since a life may literally depend upon action being taken they must be discussed.

*Bleeding*
It must be fairly obvious that unless bleeding is stopped, death will result. The basis of control of all grades of bleeding is pressure, properly applied via a suitable pad placed over the wound. Small wounds are easily controlled, larger wounds require determined pressure for a longer period – 15 to 30 minutes and then the application of a pressure dressing.

Arterial bleeding will usually respond to similar treatment, but the use of pressure points as described in the first aid manuals are a useful addition to basic direct pressure. Tourniquets alternately enjoy a vogue and are then condemned. Properly used they can be life-saving. They are applied to the upper arm and thigh only. Here there is only one bone and the tourniquet presses the underlying artery against this. There is little point in applying a tourniquet to the lower leg and forearm since the presence of the two bones makes the pressure inefficient. Tourniquets must be released every 15 to 20 minutes for a short while and whoever applied the tourniquet accepts total responsibility for its management until he passes it on to someone else. The old army trick of putting a T and the time of application on the patient's forehead is a good one. Control of bleeding from special areas is discussed adequately in the first aid manual.

*Resuscitation*
This term covers both cardiac massage and artificial respiration. Need for either or both can arise in drowning, electric shock and in people overcome by fumes. There are many other reasons but the three mentioned are the most common. The techniques are fully discussed in the manual and the diagrams are excellent. It is worth noting that the heart may still be beating even if breathing

has ceased *but* if the heart has stopped then breathing must also have ceased. Put practically, this means that one may have to apply artificial respiration alone but cardiac massage must always be accompanied by artificial respiration. The techniques are much easier than they appear at first sight and a practical demonstration is worth many words. Most St John Ambulance centres will be only too glad to demonstrate.

I have not attempted in these notes to cover all eventualities but I have tried to complement the first aid manuals by stressing the things that may be encountered on a school journey. A word about equipment may be in order.

### FIRST AID KIT
The usual type of first aid kit is useful, if expensive, but sticking plaster should be replaced by Micropore tape and tincture of iodine by Betodeine. Melolin non-adherent dressing and Tubegrip tubular elastic bandage should be added. Butterfly plasters are useful for small cuts.

### DRUGS
These are necessarily limited to proprietary preparations which may be bought without prescription. Aspirin and Paracetamol are good for all forms of pain. Cough mixtures are useful if the trip is of several days or weeks; suntan lotion, insect repellents also come to mind along with kaolin mixture for diarrhoea, etc. But I would like to add two suggestions which might not meet with universal approval.

The first involves the use of an antihistamine such as Phenargan. This is useful in a number of conditions. Its basic use is in allergic reactions such as hay fever but it is also very useful in insect bites, nettle stings and sunburn. It is very good in preventing travel sickness and can be used for its mild sedative properties before a plane flight or to help a nervous child to get to sleep when away from home. In the form of a medicine it is a very versatile drug. In the cream form it is useful for all bites and stings.

The other suggestion I would make is that on trips abroad for longish periods an antibiotic should be carried. The best is probably Erythromycin which comes both in tablet and medicine form. It is effective against a wide range of organisms and does not cause sensitivity reactions as others tend to do. Its use should be restricted to the obvious cases of tonsillitis, ear infection, bronchitis and infected cuts and boils. The other proviso is that medical aid is not likely to be available for twenty-four hours or more. Used in this way the advantages will far outweigh the theoretical disadvantages but, again, I would stress that this is a personal view and no one embarking on a trip abroad need feel ill equipped if these suggestions are not followed.

The ability to remain calm and the wisdom to know when help is necessary and how to summon it are more important than pills and potions.

Finally, remember most school trips are completed without undue incident, but it is wise to know how to tackle difficulties when they arise.

## A case study

The following case history, which actually happened, will serve to emphasize several useful points, not the least of which is the real meaning of responsibility or, as the lawyers put it *in loco parentis.* It will also introduce a technique not yet mentioned which is both simple and can be a life-saver.

Imagine a coach travelling along a motorway on the way to a Welsh seaside resort. It is full of excited children joyfully anticipating a day on the beach. Free from parental disapproval, most of them are indulging in their favourite pastime – eating. Among the many and varied items of food which are finding their way into eager mouths there are a number of oranges.

One young man has stuffed his mouth full to overflowing and, having extracted all the juice, attempts to swallow the remaining pulp. The quantity is such that he only tries to swallow half of it the first time. Normally it would be all right, but on this occasion the half that he is attempting to swallow is connected to that remaining by a piece of the skin which covers the segments.

The human swallowing mechanism is very efficient with built-in safeguards to ensure that the food goes where it is meant to – into the stomach and not into the windpipe where the effect can be disastrous. It operates perfectly when the lumps of food are free to move with the swallowing action. It is totally upset, however, when the food is not free to move, as in this case.

The happy sounds on the coach are interrupted by a very unpleasant sound – the sound of a child choking. Amid the general hubbub it is a little while before one of the teachers notices that something is amiss. Luckily she realizes what is wrong and fortunately she knows what to do. It is the work of a moment to fish out the offending orange flesh with a hooked finger and, literally seconds later, the danger is over and the child, though frightened, is little the worse for the experience. He is soon eating again but with less enthusiasm than before.

On this occasion the foreign body was easily accessible to the teacher's finger. This is not always so and when it has passed beyond reach and is blocking the air passage unconsciousness and death are very near. If the victim's lungs are full of air then he may be able to cough out the obstruction, but if the obstruction occurred just after he breathed out then the only action he is likely to attempt is to breathe in which simply makes the situation worse by further impacting the foreign body in the windpipe. Not only is he unable to breathe, but he cannot speak or call for help either. The current management in the first aid manuals is a firm thump between the shoulder blades and, when possible, turning the patient upside-down. Success or failure depend upon which forces are the stronger – those retaining the obstruction or those attempting to dislodge it. Sadly, all too often, the former win and each year many people choke to death.

But there now exists a new technique which makes a successful outcome immeasurably more likely. This involves the sudden application of pressure to the upper abdomen with the hands. This forces the diaphragm up and compresses the lungs. The resultant outrush of air causes the offending object to literally shoot from the mouth.

The pressure may be applied in several ways. If the patient is lying on his back, the operator sits astride his hips and face to face. Then the heel of one hand is placed just above the umbilicus with the other hand on top of it. Sudden sharp pressure is applied in an upward direction. One of the advantages of this technique is that if it fails the first time nothing has been lost and it may be repeated until successful. If vomiting occurs, the patient is turned on to his face.

If the patient is sitting or standing, the operator grasps him from behind and places one balled fist just above the umbilicus and the other hand over it. Again, sudden pressure is applied. This time with a pulling and squeezing action.

The victim can even use the technique on himself using his hands or some item of furniture such as the back of a chair. Used properly this technique rarely, if ever, fails. It is also useful in drowning cases to clear water from the airway prior to artificial respiration. It is a very good example of how a simple but soundly based technique can have dramatic results. I am sure that it will soon find its way into the first aid books.

There exists the theoretical possibility of damage to the ribs and the abdominal organs in untrained hands, but since the victim will die if nothing is done then it is a worthwhile risk to take.

## THE SICKNESS SYNDROME

You don't need to be a doctor to recognize the effects of travel sickness. It is devastating. Every parent hopes that his child will eventually grow out of it and there certainly can't be much fun in a trip out if it is going to be accompanied by a constant anxiety and the thought that being sick is inevitable. But the fact remains that on many a day trip, whether it be by coach to the seaside or by cruiser on the canal, a charter flight to the metropolis or a shanks' pony view of the Lake District the same possibility exists. Someone always has the capability to be sick and often at the worst time and in the most awkward places. It seems to be one of the greatest hazards against the annual pilgrimage which many children really enjoy. There are ways round the problem. You could sit on a piece of folded newspaper and believe that by some divine providence everyone would be insulated from the dreaded problem. You could dispense sickness tablets and forbid fizzy pop and ban the use of cheese sandwiches and pickled onions. But in spite of it all there is the great chance that someone will need the polythene bag or the bucket and newspapers. But don't despair too much; children have a quite remarkable recovery rate and it won't be long after his indisposition that little Billy strains his eyes to find the nearest chip-shop or Chinese take-away.

A great deal of these sickness misfortunes can be overcome by common sense. If you are hiring a coach, make sure there are seats for everyone. It is cheaper to put three on a seat but it is probably illegal and certainly uncomfortable – especially on a hot summer's day. Insist that the children do not stand up in the coach and arrange toilet and fresh-air stops along the route if it is a long one. Have you ever seen coaches stop on the motorway service areas? If you, as a civilian, are making for your quick cup of tea you probably curse them but spare a thought now for the harassed teacher who welcomes Watford Gap or Strensham rather like an Arab would praise Allah for a long-awaited oasis. If you are travelling by minibus, on the other hand, you might be quite surprised at how well the children travel and the corridor train offers unexpected health bonuses if your destination happens to be near a station. On the cross-channel ferry it seems sensible to ride on deck, if you can bear the draught, for fresh air seems to be a wonderful tonic to the shaky. But however you travel, the sickness syndrome must be considered unless the day is to be completely spoilt.

**References**
BARRELL, G. R. (1975) *Teachers and the Law* Methuen
BIRMINGHAM EDUCATION COMMITTEE (updated annually) *Notes for Guidance (Schools)* Birmingham Education Offices, Council House, Margaret Street, Birmingham B3 3BU
DES (1967) *Children and their Primary Schools* (Plowden Report) HMSO
HAIGH, G. (1974) *Out of School Activities* Pitman

Chapter 4

# The day tripper

## The scope

One advantage of the day trip is that it brings a sense of achievement upon completion. The teacher who sits at home watching television or enjoys soaking his feet after being on them all day somehow experiences a feeling of intense contentment. If the trip has gone off without a hitch he is almost entitled to feel that 'God's in His heaven and all's right with the world'. The problem in writing about day trips and the day tripper is that there is such a tremendous range of activities which come within the orbit of discussion. Categories vary from a visit to a museum or historic home where 'best clothes' and tidiness are the order of the day, to a tramp across open fields or through swampy woodland open to the elements, where hardship and initiative take their toll of the weak and inadequate. It is of little consolation to advise a young teacher that he or she must choose the trip so that it is appropriate to the needs and interests of the children concerned but, as a general rule, the young children will be pleased with the zoo and playgrounds whilst the teenagers will want a challenge for both mind and body. It is useful to keep a record of trips which have been successful and to share the details with colleagues in other schools: it is also sensible to discuss intended trips with the children concerned. They are hardly likely to enjoy a trip to the Ironbridge Gorge – however well organized – if they have been there twice before. Children are surprisingly resilient and will respond to the demands of a day trip which would be too rigorous for many adults. It is better to do too much than to find the children are bored by lunch time because the adventure is over. In such a setting lie the ingredients for trouble and disaster. School Travel of Cardiff advertise a 'new day trip to France' with the following itinerary:

Convenient departure by coach from your school to Southampton. Transfer of coach and party to Townsend Cross Channel Ferry. 23.00 hours depart Southampton: 07.30 hours arrive Le Havre. Party and coach disembark at Le Havre to continue on whole-day coach tour along the French coast visiting such places as Caen, Bayeux, Carenton and then continuing to Cherbourg. Stops for sightseeing. At Cherbourg transfer of coach and party to ferry for return Cross Channel sailing. 17.30 hours depart Cherbourg. 21.30 hours arrive Southampton and then continue by coach to your school.

It sounds quite a marathon, and even the promise of a free trip for one teacher with every fifteen children might fail to tempt many teachers, yet it opens up new possibilities and vistas and makes a visit to the nearest seaside resort seem more than a little tame. Tired children might be grisly and obstreperous but they are hardly likely to rush off and find trouble. One school in the West Midlands recently proved the efficacy of intense activity. Two members of staff, driving a borrowed minibus, drove at speed up to the Lake District. Their lively pupils climbed some of the highest crags, sought out fossils and rock samples, cooked a meal in the open air and returned home by about 10.30 pm, having enjoyed a sixteen-hour day. The parents were surprised at the stamina and the quietness when their sons came home safely and made straight for bed – in spite of the temptation of *Match of The Day*.

But this is not to say that distance and activity equate proportionately with success. The destination and what it offers is very often of more importance than the mileage. Day trips should offer excitement, pleasure and fellowship in keeping with the age and curiosity of the children. Sometimes this thrill can be realized by a new form of travel. In these days of car travel it is quite an event for some children to see a train, a boat or a pony and very often a 'return to nature' brings unexpected pleasures to town children. An enterprising teacher can create days out which do not cost a great deal once the transport problem has been settled. This was true when the author visited the Oxfordshire village of Hook Norton recently. Ten children and two teachers travelled by minibus from the city into the unknown. After a short stop *en route* to obey the calls of nature they arrived in a pretty country spot. There was a visit to one of the oldest breweries in the country, a lunch-time meeting with some of the local inhabitants including the village bard, and a walk over the disused railway viaduct and through an empty, eerie tunnel. What an opportunity for creative English and what an experience for youngsters. The church provided the tangible signs of history, with its plaques and tombs and a chance for brass rubbings, and the journey introduced the idea of navigation, direction and road sense. All this, plus a game on the swings and slides in the park, meant a successful day. It cost the children almost nothing and the headteacher just the petrol money. Yet it probably gave as much in terms of experience to the children who went there as a far more expensive and sophisticated commercial trip would have done.

Perhaps the best way of giving help and advice on the day trip theme is to put forward some examples of trips which, though different, were equally satisfactory for those who enjoyed them. It is important to remember that each trip was a 'product of its time' – in a sense, a unique occasion. This is not to say that it will not offer suggestions which are valuable as a source of inspiration or emulation.

**A ramble along the Severn**
A ramble has the advantage of being a cheap day out once the group has got to its starting point. To make transportation easier it is a wise move to arrange the walk so that it begins and ends at the same place. The description which follows refers to a ramble along the River Severn at Bewdley in Worcestershire. It is reproduced exactly in the same note and diagram form as it was recorded in the teacher's log-book at the time. The reader may consider that this Boy Scout method of reporting can stand in its own right. Such a log, suitably illustrated, would be excellent as a resource for others who contemplated the same journey at a later date.

| Time | Description, events etc. | Sketch map |
|---|---|---|
| 11.09 | Twenty-four children, two guides, left town car park at Bewdley; turned left into main street. Proceeded towards the river. Traffic heavy. Quite hot. | |
| 11.12 | Turned left and began leisurely walk along the riverside. Noticed a rowing crew at | |

practice with coxswain.
Tommy Brown led the way.

11.33  Stopped at disused railway
bridge and watched man trying
to beat the current in a small
boat with an outboard motor.
No sign of the church marked
on the map. Stream enters the
river at this point.

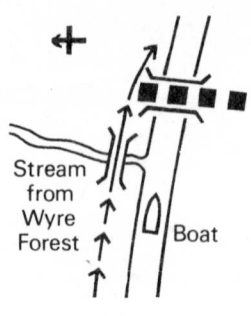

Stream from Wyre Forest

Boat

On up river, passing cottage on
left, to stile. Over the stile.
Wyre Forest to left, through
field with cows. Interesting
river silt.

12.08  Along small muddy pathway,
through a gate and on towards
Arley. Wet and overgrown
riverside path. Willow trees.

12.16  Through small swing gate.
Orchard to our left and massive
aqueduct ahead. Freshly
painted. Short rest here for
lunch. Sounds of gun shot.
Tidy up.

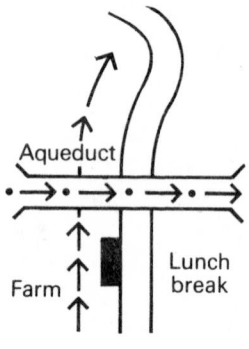

Aqueduct

Farm

Lunch break

12.40  No litter. Onwards over stile
and into barley field. Gate.

12.45  Sign of a new reservoir to our
right on the other side of the
river. A splendid wooded
region, passing along forested
paths. Quite dark in places.

13.00  Emerging from wooded path.
Over stile.

13.03  Railway bridge in view over
stile. At the Victoria Bridge – a
product of the Coalbrookdale
iron works. Take a photo.

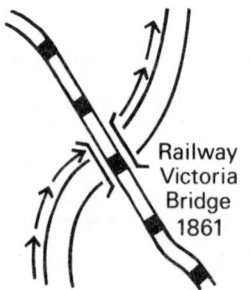

Railway Victoria Bridge 1861

13.10  Over another stile. Round the
edge of a field with mixed
crops. Lettuce and potato.

13.18  Through gate and up to the
river crossing at Arley.
Boarded ferry to cross river.

The ferryman spoke of difficulties he had in moving vessel across the river using only tiller and cables.

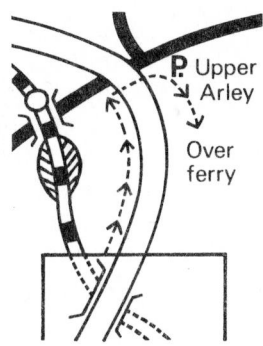

13.30   Off Ferry. Here was the local post office. A Mecca for ice creams and lemonade. It looked like rain. Kim and Karen were very tired.

13.40   After a short break the return journey began along the other side of the river. Through a woodland area where a sign says 'Birmingham Anglers Association' – on to a stile which we crossed and skirted meadow taking top path and passing telegraph poles leading to Arley village.

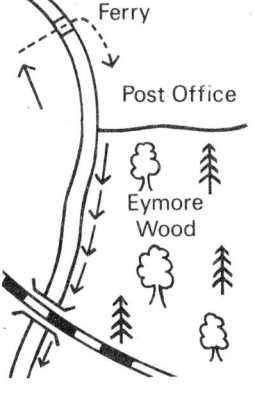

13.47   Over yet another stile and along a dark, secluded woodland path. The ground was still very muddy as we followed path to the base of the railway bridge.

Under bridge and up hill. Following the broad expanse of the river. On the left are foothills of the new reservoir.

14.05   Up to look at reservoir. Noticed a really big horse chestnut tree with signs of growing fruits.

Coming down steep slopes of reservoir to bridle-path we passed a sign to Bewdley. It is necessary to turn left behind a cottage to find the very muddy riverside path again.

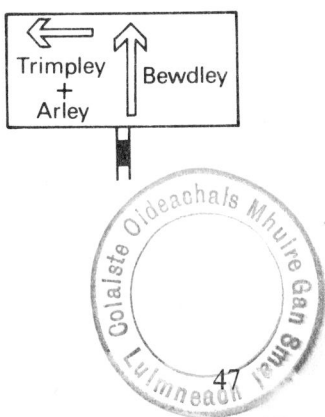

14.20   Quagmire. Who can manage to stand up?

14.22   Over wooden sleepers in path to bridge and further stile. Bear left up metalled path to aqueduct. Pipes – three of them – are here covered in – leaving only inspection covers. Railway to our left. River, but no riverside path to our right.

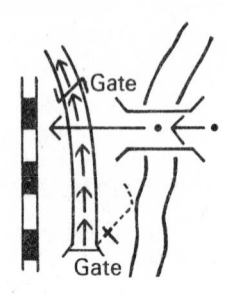

14.30     Through gate, shutting it behind us, and on down metalled path. Evidence of weekend and summer hideaways.

14.40     Station up to the left. Phone box in distance. Continue to walk along the road. Good walk.

14.45     Cross fence into field with cows and down again to river's edge.

14.55     Cross under bridge using ledge along the parapet with our 'backs to the wall'. Under oak trees along the river path to a 'launch pad' and ramp with a hut where there is a cable which crosses the river. (This, we are advised, is for measuring the depth and volume of water in the river.)

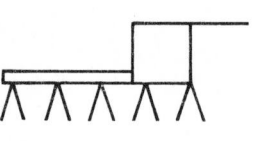

15.05     Over stile and along the riverside again. Eventually the path turns sharp left behind bungalows and rowing club house. Bewdley is visible over river to the right.

         On to track. Canoes and club boats on racks to our left.

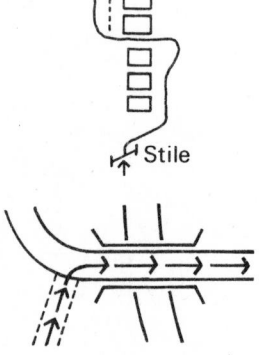

15.18     Car showroom on the right. Town bridge and almost our journey's end.

         Quite a strenuous trip for town children. Yet they seemed to have enjoyed it.

## Repeating the golden rule

The actual details of the ramble, whether it be over the Clent Hills or along the River Severn, are not as important as the fact that it actually took place. But what the teacher must remember is that the route had been investigated before the children set out. 'Teacher goes first' is the golden rule for all day trips where there is any chance of meeting the unexpected. Maps can be very much out of date and it is no good relying entirely on the relevant Ordnance Survey map for paths, routes and information. Guide-books can also be misleading and facts can change from year to year. If it is impossible for the teacher in charge to visit the site, venue or destination reasonably near to the time of the trip, then it might be thought sensible to change the outing into something less uncertain. Teachers can't afford to be reckless and leave things to chance, hoping like Mr Micawber that something might just turn up to save their bacon.

If the visit planned is a highly organized one to a museum, or a historic building then there may be some excuse for not going there beforehand – but only if the programme is in the hands of the organizers whose own experienced education staff are used to dealing with school parties. Teachers should never turn up unannounced with parties of children. It is necessary to make firm arrangements in advance. Apart from the sheer courtesy involved, this prevents a major catastrophe when there are too many visitors and not enough staff to accommodate them satisfactorily. The same principle holds good whether the venue is The British Museum, The Tate Gallery or the local library or museum. Teachers should try to cement good public relations rather than destroy them.

Having visited a place before, the teacher knows roughly what is in store for the children. If the trip is to be in the open air – and many of the summer term trips fall into this category – then it will be necessary to take note of the terrain and the possible effects of bad weather. Try to avoid taking children up Snowdon in sandals or being caught out by a cloudburst in the country with nowhere to shelter and no waterproof clothing. If the trip includes an overnight stop then a whole new range of expectations will need to be catered for in a clothing list. Remember the Boy Scouts' motto to 'Be Prepared'.

On a visit to Hampshire and the New Forest some lively city children were addressed by a local headmaster. Before they went into the forest he gave them some advice: 'When you go into the forest take only one thing – fresh air – and leave absolutely nothing.' Teachers should think carefully about the taking of specimens. Living things very often become dead things when they are removed from their natural habitat and wantonly removing plants, insects, fish and animals does little to advance the cause of conservation. The same idea may be applied to the collection of samples, pamphlets and various printed items: one or two souvenirs for a group scrap-book or a project report may be considered reasonable, but it is wasteful and wrong to acquire material which will then be lost, thrown away or used to litter the coach or train on the way home.

The problem of conservation is becoming so important that the Council for Environmental Education had this to say in its *Report on Field Party Leadership* (1975):

> The knocking down of wire fences and stone walls, the damaging of gates and the scaring of animals all add to the farmers' and landowners' dislike of field parties. It has been suggested that landowners may well close their lands to field study groups unless parties are properly controlled. Many geological sites have been needlessly battered by students. The Nature Conservancy has also designated certain areas as Sites of Special Scientific Interest to which access is limited and the British Geomorphological Research Group is compiling a list of sites of Special Geomorphological Interest to which access will again be limited. In the Home Counties members of the National Farmers' Union have been advised not to allow schools to visit their farms. The use of questionnaires is also becoming a problem in favoured field study areas and arouses the antagonism of the local inhabitants. In one town the Chamber of Commerce complained bitterly to the Education Authority about the problem of the numerous school parties that were conducting shopping price surveys. It may well be that much of the data collection and sampling for the modern geography could be done by a small number of people and the results made available for other groups.

So the golden rule of 'teacher goes first' ought really to be rephrased in its wider connotation that 'teacher takes the initiative'. The teacher not only has to know where he is going and what difficulties have to be overcome: he also has to ensure that certain standards of behaviour and concern are going to be maintained by the children. It is a daunting prospect for those who are contemplating being 'out and about' for the first time but, once trained, children will generally respond to the standards which the staff impose. An example of this could be taken from a recent trip to Europe. As soon as the children left the cross-channel ferry and boarded their coach, the driver laid down his own version of the law with regard to litter and keeping the coach clean. There was to be no eating and the driver was so firm, friendly and efficient that even the 'biggest tearaway' in the party wouldn't chance his luck and sweets were left safely tucked away in duffle bags.

## On the water

Britain has an extensive network of inland waterways and many parts of the country have direct access to the canals which once vied with the railway as the most important commercial arteries. In recent years much of the mess and dereliction has been cleared – often by voluntary effort on the part of enthusiasts – and there is now a popular trend towards seeing the country from the deck or cabin of a canal barge. In arranging such a trip teachers will almost certainly be at the mercy of the commercial firms who make their boats available for charter. In Birmingham the Brummagem Trip Boats offer a choice of journeys:

S1   A two-hour trip to Winson Green and return, including Icknield Port Road Wharf Loop and Oozells Street Loop
S2   A three-hour trip to Smethwick Junction and return, including a half-hour stop to walk up Smethwick Locks
S3   A three-hour trip to Selly Oak and return
S4   A seven-hour trip to Hopwood and Bittel Reservoirs and return
S5   A seven-hour trip to Windmill End at Dudley and return.

These organized trips include a half-hour talk in the Gas Street Basin Museum which is a useful introduction to canal cruising, and the boats which carry the passengers have tuck shop, bar, music and toilet facilities on board. Teachers should not be deterred by the Conditions of Charter included in small print on the programme, for the canal outing is a very useful way of organizing a class trip. Perhaps the greatest stumbling block is making sure that the transport to and from the canal basin is fixed with a reliable coach company who won't forget the prearranged pick-up and set-down times.

Not to be outdone, Merseyside Transport organizes Teach-in Tours aboard the *Royal Daffodil*. For a small fee, pupils receive an explanatory booklet with a map of the Mersey and surrounding area and a two-hour tour of one of the world's most famous ports. The organizers are probably right when they claim that such a teach-in cruise will make geography, history or science come alive for children of all ages.

Privately arranged trips on the inland waterways may be a great deal harder to arrange and the teacher will need to look out for the legal pitfalls and implications of taking children off *terra firma*.

BRITISH WATERWAYS BOARD

The Press and Publicity Office offers the following information on inland waterways:

The canals of Britain are increasingly in the news, and in fact they provide one of the most fascinating topics for children of all ages to study. The history and development of our inland waterways is an exciting study in itself, but the canal system as it exists today is equally absorbing. Not only have there been new developments in transport by water on the broad canals, but the whole waterway system is entering on an era of use by a wider public.

The British Waterways Board own and manage some 3,000 kilometres of inland waterways and their associated supply reservoirs. Several hundred kilometres are still used primarily for the transport of freight: all are available for the pleasure and interest of the general public. While angling and cruising have been popular for many years, an increasing number of people are using the towing paths for rambling and nature study. The wealth of plants and flowers present, even in industrial areas such as Birmingham, amazes the newcomer. Canals are unique in that they provide an opportunity not only to examine their natural history, but also to illustrate transport history, communications, eighteenth- and nineteenth-century architecture and industrial archaeology.

The narrow boat, locks, tunnels and weirs, which are all part of a working canal system, also provide excellent opportunities for first-hand study. More and more schools now make actual journeys on canals and some – including primary schools – have boats of their own. Teachers will scarcely need to be reminded of the necessity to instruct children in the risks that are inherent in the fascinations of water areas. On the canals locks are among the most obvious places of potential danger, but it has also to be recognized that the water immediately alongside the towing path may sometimes be quite deep. With young children – and with older children if they have not yet been taught to swim – it is vital that they be accompanied by a responsible adult.

The British Waterways Board have a large number of leaflets on aspects of canals. Their Code of Conduct (free with s.a.e.) has humorous drawings to show how to cruise canals and operate locks. The paperback *Waterway User's Companion* (75p including postage) is full of information about waterways, including line drawings and lists of hire firms and boating clubs. The Board also publish attractive posters and postcards. Write to British Waterways Board, Melbury House, Melbury Terrace, London NW1 6JX.

More addresses for information and permits are given at the end of this chapter.

For most landlubbers a trip on the water, be it canal or river, opens up new experiences and it might be a wise move to do some background reading before the journey. An excellent book for this purpose is *Holiday Cruising on Inland Waterways* by Hadfield and Streat (1971). It gives a great deal of useful information for the uninitiated travellers, and in trying to express the pleasures to be gained from boating one of the authors writes:

Who can define or explain the enjoyment of a boat on water, on the Broads, a river or a canal? Of course it's not idyllic. Sometimes it rains. Things can go wrong with the boat . . . Things can get wrapped round the propeller. But there are the times when it doesn't rain, the early mornings when the mist lies over the land and the wind ripples the water ahead, and through a bridge hole one can see the uptilted beams of a lock. The smell of coffee and frying bacon; waving to passengers in a parallel train; rides given to children from a passing car, returned to their bewildered parents at the next bridge; lying on deck and lazily watching the trees' shadows;

having time to look at flowers and plants, birds and animals; and at night returning from a walk along the towpath to see the cabin lights shining on the water.

It is important to remember that the towpath of a canal is not a public right of way and each teacher should find out the regulations applicable to his party when they are contemplating a canal trip. Some education authorities have negotiated agreements with British Waterways Board for organized visits to canal property but permission must be sought by individual parties to make sure that their trip meets with official approval. Teachers should be particularly cautious about signing forms of indemnity which absolve the Board of all responsibility for personal injury or damage to property. By so doing they could contravene the accepted procedure laid down by their own local authority. If in doubt, find out.

**Travel by rail**
There are certain obvious features which make rail travel appear advantageous. Children can move about. There are toilet and restaurant facilities and a chance to meet other people on the journey. The one drawback comes if the points of arrival and departure are not exactly in the same place as the railway station. But in terms of speed and comfort a journey which is inter-city in nature might be best achieved on the railway.

British Rail offer special terms to school parties and can arrange for special trains or even charter trips. The best way to summarize this is to reproduce below part of a letter which the author received from the London Midland Region offices of British Rail in response to a request for information:

Dear Sir
I enclose for information a copy of my letter which was sent to most schools in this area earlier in the year.

The basic problem I have in promulgating information about juvenile parties stems from the fact that providing the party number requirement, *viz* ten juveniles travelling together, is met this facility is available between any two stations on British Rail. Except for very local journeys savings are appreciable and of course the juvenile fare quoted applies to the actual number travelling (subject to the

10 minimum) not a guaranteed number that will be needed to fill a coach. The reductions are given in relation to day and period tickets.

Charter train arrangements are available for anyone and schools do take advantage of them, but to be able to bring the fare down you would need at least 400 children travelling. Charter train charges are based on the current costs and in consequence fluctuate but given date of travel, type of train, destination etc., firm quotes are given. At the present time a train with 420 seats Birmingham to Rhyl would cost £590. I would add that if small children are involved, by seating four a side in each compartment instead of three, the same train could accommodate approximately 150 more juveniles. It is appreciated that the charter arrangement generally is not much used for schools because it does necessitate such large numbers and in consequence during the summer months we operate a number of School Party Special trains. This enables smaller schools to book parties for which we arrange reservations on the train.

Arrangements required for meals, local tours, steamers, admission to zoos etc. are undertaken by our staff and no charge is made for this service subject, of course, to the party travelling by rail.

With such a helpful portfolio how could a teacher overlook the claims of rail travel? If the price is right and the timetable appropriate then the locomotive must be superior in speed and comfort to the coach! But, at any rate, it is worth contacting British Rail to see if they can offer suitable arrangements for that day trip.

**Up in the air**
In the age of Concorde it is quite surprising to see what little use schools make of air travel, especially as it is so quick and efficient. One inner-ring school arranged a flight to London, a trip round the airport and a coach trip back home. Not a bad day out, including the experience of flying like a bird! To make the trip a viable proposition in terms of cost, it was arranged that a neighbouring school should share the facilities. They travelled to the metropolis by coach and returned home on the same aircraft that brought their neighbours. The trip was arranged through a small company and, at the time of writing, British Airways show

little response to suggestions that they might emulate their smaller competitors. But there can be little doubt that a flight is, of itself, a very useful experience and one in which, ideally, every child ought to be able to participate.

## That coach trip

The flexibility of the coach trip makes it number one choice with most teachers. In spite of the heat, the traffic jams, the sickness syndrome and escalating costs the coach has one great advantage. All the children can be kept together and taken from school to the destination and back again. There is less chance of losing anyone *en route* (although one school returning from Bristol Zoo did gain a quiet little girl who hadn't noticed she was on the wrong coach) and it is relatively easy to supervise the children.

But one word of warning needs to be sounded on medium distance trips. The coach companies like to keep their vehicles on the road earning money and so they try to fit school trips in between their regular commitments. This can mean that the teacher's arrangements will have to be subjugated to the coach company's obligations. It is important to make it clear that your time of starting back is to be as stated in the initial booking unless you want your trip ruined by a driver who insists that he has another job to do and that you must start back earlier than planned.

It would be impossible to describe the range of coach trips which can be planned. Suffice it to say that the coach has the advantage over other forms of transport in that it can stop and start and go wherever your own special itinerary demands. This makes it ideal for a day outing which takes in more than one port of call. It is useful to have a map and a clear idea of where you want to go just in case the driver happens to be on supply and is unaware of your special requirements. Talk to the driver, cooperate with him, invite him to the picnic and, if you are pleased, tell him so. Once some hooligans threw a stone through the windscreen of a coach: the driver managed to pull up; the children and staff piled into the following coach to come back to school. In gratitude the headteacher wrote to the coach company to compliment the driver's action. It cost nothing but the postage. It was an act of gratitude and courtesy. But both the driver and the operators appreciated that their services had been gratefully received.

A reminder to the teacher: check the luggage rack for your own camera and umbrella. It's a long way to the bus station, especially if you've never beer there before and you don't know where it is!

**Ten tips for trips**
Doreen Gower, an experienced and enthusiastic tripper, offers the following ten tips for successful trips:

1　Always have an aim as well as the enjoyment. It might be a topic for study such as transport, housing, costume, industries etc.
2　Provide the children with booklets or worksheets so that they can record what they see. List things to notice and compile a number of questions to make sure that they gain something from the trip.
3　Do the trip yourself–don't rely upon what others say. Things can change in quite a short time so cover the ground yourself as close to the date of the trip as possible.
4　Check the route with the coach company regarding the places of note *en route*. Make sure that if more than one coach is used they have the same route plan. (It has been known for three coaches on the same trip to have three different routes.)
5　Ensure that there are adequate toilet and refreshment facilities. If children are taking sandwiches find out where they can eat them if the weather should be wet.
6　Make full use of local museum and library services when planning your trips. Their help can be invaluable.
7　Contact local historical groups in the area to be visited, e.g. Old Handsworth Society, Friends of Ironbridge, Severn Valley Railway.
8　It is essential to have a timetable: but do have a fairly flexible one so that plans can be altered if necessary.
9　Make sure children are in smallish groups with a reliable leader. Most places suggest fifteen children to a group, though ten is better if the staff can be found!
10　Do plan the trip so that the children can have enjoyment as well as education and try to finish on the former so that the children don't realize that they have been working. They like to take small gifts home for their family so check that there are gifts available and at reasonable prices.

It might sound like common sense, but years of experience are behind these words of wisdom!

## Useful addresses

*Waterways history*
The Waterways Museum, Stoke Bruerne, Nr Towcester, Northamptonshire NN12 7SE

*Canal shops and information centres*
Waterways Museum Shop, Stoke Bruerne, Nr Towcester, Northamptonshire NN12 7SE
Canal Shop and Information Centre, 2 Kingston Row, Birmingham B1 2NU
Canal Shop, Chester Road, Nantwich, Cheshire
Canal Office, Delamere Terrace, Paddington, London W2 6ND
Caledonian Canal Office, Clachnaharry, Inverness IV3 6RA
Inland Waterways Association, 114 Regents Park Road, London NW1 8UQ

## References
COUNCIL FOR ENVIRONMENTAL EDUCATION (1975) *Report of the Schools Committee Working Party on Field Party Leadership* Council for Environmental Education, School of Education, University of Reading, 24 London Road, Reading RG1 5AQ
HADFIELD, C. and STREAT, M. (1971) *Holiday Cruising on Inland Waterways* David and Charles

# Chapter 5

# Communing with nature

Our children live in the nuclear age. Television, computers, satellites and transplant surgery are commonplace: *The Six Million Dollar Man*, with his bionic limbs and infra-red scanning equipment is the latest folk hero. To some people it may seem sinister that Dracula and Frankenstein have been replaced by Steve Austin and yet such a character is not so far from reality as many may think. As the television narrator says, 'We have the technology to rebuild' and the end-product will almost certainly be better than the original.

The strange thing is that for many of our children the leisure age means the age of instant entertainment – switch on the television and you are set for the rest of the day. Perhaps it's a part of what was once referred to as our affluent society. If the television breaks down the drug is gone and the relative peace of the home is shattered by the new demands of boredom.

It is quite refreshing, therefore, to write about some people's genuine attempts to redress the balance by taking children away from school and into the country or the seaside where they can learn all about living the more spartan life under canvas. Many primary schools now run a regular school camp as a part of their character building scheme. There's absolutely nothing new about the idea. All through history men have found it necessary to commune with nature and many educational schemes have looked upon camping as an essential training in initiative and resourcefulness. The instructor Nigel Hunt (1969) phrased it neatly in his book when he said:

Man has camped since the Dark Ages in caves and holes, under skins, pelts and hides, below wattle, bamboo, palm leaves, inside snow holes, ice crannies and hollow trees, in

59

the lee of rocks, outcrops, hedges or his horse. Every cover from parachutes to aeroplane's life raft dragged on to an ice floe has been a part of 'camping'.

But, although camping has widened the curriculum and emphasized the quality of life, it has brought schools problems in terms of finance and staffing. Introducing young children to the thrills and demands of life in the open is no easy task and teachers need enthusiasm and physical stamina if they are to reach their objectives. 'Passenger teachers' are of no use to the organizer of a camping experience for normal lively children. They must go off alone if they want to escape the 'rat race' of life.

**Roughing it**

Many people equate the idea of camping with living rough. If their experiences have been unhappy ones, then this is understandable. In a force nine gale, overlooking Barmouth Bay, when the tent is packed underneath all the other equipment and the children are arguing about nothing, tempers can become frayed and the sport of camping loses its attraction. Camping in poor weather conditions is one of the surest ways of undermining morale, and institutionalized camping of the kind envisaged when thirty or more children are involved can quickly take its toll of the inexperienced. A wet Welsh weekend demands tolerance, perseverence and a sense of humour. But, if the preparation has been properly done and the equipment is more than adequate, then there is no need for teachers and children to 'rough it' at camp. Somewhere between the image of a one-man bivouac made from a polythene sheet held by ropes and meat skewers and the colourful and sophisticated view of a village of canvas, trailers and geometric frame tents, fitted with sinks and electrics, lies the security and comfort of the schools' standing camp.

The best way to answer the criticism that camping is only for the hardy is to try and describe what happens in a typical schools' annual camping expedition. As Barmouth Bay has been mentioned it seems appropriate to use the Talybont campsite as an example. Here, year by year, the staff and children of Yenton Junior School and Marsh Hill Primary School set about trying to achieve the benefits which stem from acquiring that 'natural balance between mental and physical striving'. The notes which follow relate to the 1972 campaign which was a joint venture between the two schools – an experiment in cooperation rather than competition.

TO CAMP WE GO

It was a cold February night when the staff of the two schools first met to discuss their strategies and plans for a combined camp in mid Wales. The meeting was quite informal, with coffee and biscuits and plenty of shared gossip, but it gave all the staff, their wives, husbands and boyfriends the chance to get to know each other – some to renew old acquaintances, others to meet for the first time. The spirit of working together for the common good was to be the theme of the exercise.

It was decided that the camping party should consist of forty-five children: half from each school and twelve 'teachers'. There were more staff from Marsh Hill and more children from Yenton – which only serves to stress the aspect of working together. The leaders were the author of these notes and Mr V. R. Watson, Head of Marsh Hill School, and the democratic ideals of the majority were never subjugated to autocracy in the combined venture.

In the event the camp was marked by a spirit of cooperation. Initiative, happiness and common sense prevailed. Joint ventures like this have little scope for the *prima donna* and, as was said in the introduction, passengers on the staff are most definitely not required. Give and take, with an emphasis on the giving, are the ingredients for success.

By mid-June most of the money had been collected and banked in a special camp account and the bulk of the food – large catering size tins – had been purchased from a city 'cash and carry'. Arrangements had been made in a preliminary visit to purchase perishable goods – bread, meat, milk etc – from a local supplier. At the same time an agreement had been made with the nearby garage owner to supply the 'official camp vehicles' with fuel when they had reached Talybont. The farmer who owned the site had been visited and a check made to see if there were any changes needed from the established routine. For instance, where would the toilets be dug? What special equipment would be needed for water supplies? Where can the accompanying vehicles be parked during the camp period? Hand in hand with these preparations had gone the administrative necessities: consent forms, insurance and medical inspections had all been dealt with in turn.

61

Collecting together sufficient equipment is, in itself, quite a mammoth undertaking. The schools had built up their own stock over the years, adding, perhaps, one or two new items each year with any profits left in the funds, and scrounging tents and other items from kind parents and do-gooders. The camp store, under the stairs in an old stockroom, was easily accessible for loading and unloading and resembled Aladdin's cave by the variety and quantity of its many treasures. But it was still necessary to borrow items from the education authority's central stores. These were requisitioned early in the school year and would be available on the day required. Transporting them to and from the stores was an added responsibility. The point to remember is that one can never have too many tents when the camp party totals over sixty. It is wise to err on the side of generosity when allocating tent space, and tents which were capable of accommodating six generally had no more than three occupants. On this particular expedition there were about twenty tents. They varied in size and shape from Continental frame tents and Stormhavens to inflatable igloos and an American Army marquee. The old marquee took some erecting for teachers who were not used to the circus, but it served well as a dining room and cookhouse, and as a social centre in the long evenings.

One feature of this camp was the practice of sending an advance party to Talybont to prepare the site for the bulk of the campers who would arrive the next day. Two vans were hired from a large rental company at what seemed to be a competitive rate and two members of staff – one from each school – took a van each, loaded with the bulk of the food and other equipment and seven likely lads, on the long drive through Shrewsbury and Welshpool and Dolgelly to the coast. It was a pity that one of the vehicles, a Morris J4, was so badly maintained that it broke down on the mountain road but bottles of lemonade helped to cool the deprived engine and the Bedford van took on more cargo as the small convoy limped the last ten miles to the campsite. During the time of the camp these two vans were used for transporting children, for ferrying luggage and collecting wood and supplies. There were four drivers insured to drive these and during the course of the camp each of the four drove both vehicles and by mutual agreement either 'rode shotgun' or stayed at camp when their skills were not required. Luckily, under this arrangement nobody ever felt compelled to go anywhere simply because a driver was needed and he was the only one available. It is wise to have sufficient driver-teachers in the party so that every possible contingency is covered.

The advance party worked hard. Pits were dug, latrines and toilets erected and the equipment, which had been brought on a separate lorry, was unloaded and sorted out. By the time the rest of the campers arrived on the following day, at about three o'clock, the bulk of the work had been done and the celebration stew was beginning to simmer in the makeshift kitchen.

Imagine the scene on that day when forty children are suddenly set free from an excessively warm coach after what, to them, has seemed an endless journey. They see green fields, trees, holidaymakers, tents and caravans. They smell the sea air and hear the river roaring in full flight down its course. Each and every sense quivers with eager expectation. This is it. For half an hour their kit, which was so carefully packed at home by loving hands ceases to have any meaning or value and off they explode to take the air and explore their new base for the very first time. Meanwhile in a last tired fervour of determination the teachers drink that cup of tea and sort out their priorities. 'Thank God it's not raining,' says one and the others give a silent assent to that cherished thought.

At moments like this one is thankful that the preparation has been well done. A cottage tent serves as a temporary store for luggage and items of equipment. It will take at least a day to sort everything out into its proper place. To use the overworked phrase: there should be a place for everything and everything should be in its place. That's the way to camp.

But think of those happy children for a moment. It may be that some of them have never left home before. They are excited and they will find it hard to make any decisions. So don't expect them to. Organize them and settle them down into the new way of life. The first night will seem endless and few, if any, of the staff, let alone the children, will get any sleep. Flashes of tired torches and snatches of whispered conversation will keep the tent patrol busy until the small hours. Understanding, kindness and tolerance will be necessary as the young campers are introduced to the discipline of living under canvas. On the second night it will be a different story and by then the children will be so tired that they will want to sleep anyway.

**Organizing the programme**

As with most activities of an educational nature things just can't be left to happen. There must be a sense of purpose and a strong framework of order within the camp community.

Let's pick up the story of the 1972 Talybont camp again. The children were grouped into six squads and these were numbered alphabetically from A to F. Each group took its turn to carry out the following duties under the watchful eye of its adult leader: water and field clearing; morning washing-up and marquee; evening washing up; sandwiches and kitchen utensils; potato peeling and standby squad. In addition to this the staff were divided into two sections X and Y. These would take it in turns to get up early, to help the cook and to serve the meals. Every successful camp needs the sort of cook who is prepared to be married to the kitchen and our camp was fortunate indeed to have such a jewel in Bernard Grainger. Working what seemed to be an eighteen-hour day, he was always in attendance, using his own skill, planning and initiative so that the staff only had to worry about the children and not the meals. But this system of organization worked very well and by sharing out the jobs every child and adult was directly involved in running the expedition.

A daily routine is essential. Each morning after breakfast the daily chores were dealt with. Potatoes were well and truly peeled, water containers filled and refilled, wood supplies gathered, sandwiches cut, supplies topped up, toilets emptied and the sick parade attended to. The usual scratches, bites and burns were well within the capability of the staff. Doubtful cases were taken in to the nearest doctor and one girl's cut had to be stitched at the local hospital. Around midday the sandwiches were eaten, crisps and apples were consumed and the topic of conversation veered towards the programme for the rest of the day. Usually a choice of afternoon activities were offered. These were many and varied and, on occasions, some children opted to stay on the campsite away from the 'madding crowd'. There was, then, this flexibility according to supply and demand. Some of the better afternoons derived from a spontaneous suggestion rather than from intensive preplanning. Such an experience was the trip to Towyn, a ride on the Talyllyn Railway and the walk to Dolgoch Falls: quite a happy and stimulating experience for town children.

For the record, the options explored on this particular trip included the following:

A visit to Harlech Castle and the sand dunes with swimming and fun and games on the beach; a trip through Dolgelly to the foot of Cader Idris and a very strong walk to the summit and back; into Barmouth by van, then a walk over the railway bridge and over the sand dunes to Fairbourne and back on the miniature railway to cross the estuary by boat; a ride to Shell Island where time was spent pottering about in those rock pools and looking at aircraft on the way; a walk up through the woods from camp to a wonderful inland lake in the hills where one could really commune with nature and the hardy could enjoy an invigorating swim; afternoons spent on the beach enjoying the conventional seaside fare – with slot machines; a short drive to the sand dunes of Duffryn for 'desert campaign games or simple sunbathing'; an afternoon spent in Barmouth, buying those presents and sticks of rock, and a trip through Forestry Commission Land to the Welsh Gold Mine.

The trips have to be considered in terms of their length and their cost. Sometimes a wide game in the camp environs will be more welcome than an expensive outing to, say, Conway Castle or Snowdon. The camp leaders will need to sense the demand, bearing in mind that keen and eager teachers will make any trip a success if they believe in it. By the same token they can ruin, even if unwittingly, a project in which they have little faith and no enthusiasm. The evenings in camp saw the channelling of that boundless enthusiasm of youth into cricket, football, hide and seek, chess, reading, bingo and quizzes in the marquee. Children want to be constantly doing things and the staff need to be on their mettle to keep them going until time for cocoa and lights out.

The evening meal was, traditionally, the best one of the day and the bill for butcher's meat, chops, faggots and pies was quite heavy. One of the great favourites was stew followed by jelly, fruit and cream. Few children could manage more than two helpings of this fare but nearly everyone managed to find room for at least one helping of seconds. The author once had two helpings of both dinner and sweet: but next day had to pay the penalty of greed and visit the chemist's for stomach medicine.

Each day brought its own wealth of experiences for staff and children alike. Words cannot express the relationships which existed and the feeling of fellowship which was engendered. It is said that you don't know a person until you have lived with them, and many children gained quite simply from having to live with

E

someone new, if only for a short time. It is a credit to the staff and children that the spirit and ethos of the camp was undeniably happy.

**Financial considerations**

In terms of finances the Talybont camp was a great success. Each child paid £12.50 and this covered all the costs. The twelve-day camp with all its food, the journey by coach from Birmingham, the hire of two vans, trips, petrol and incidental expenses, insurance, the hire of a lorry to move a mountain of equipment and kit, emergency costs such as a burst tyre or a medical prescription – all of these were met from the global sum of £560. The fact that we were solvent was due in no small measure to the expert buying of the quartermaster, and the chef's carefully planned menus. Anyone who is contemplating such a venture would be well advised to buy their supplies in the big city and take them with them into the country.

There is a provocative feature to the discussion of camp finances. To run a camp on the lines described, providing entertainment, transport, first-class food and every known safeguard, one needs a certain basic monetary requirement in addition to adequate staffing. The resources of the two schools made this possible, but it is doubtful whether one school working alone could achieve such standards. The break-even point comes with about forty children and a dozen staff, and few schools could find that many children and adults keen to give up a fortnight of their long holiday in order that such a scheme might take place.

**Must we be so adventurous?**

In a paper written for a book on environmental studies, V. R. Watson (1976) wrote the following words:

A large field, flat and well drained, flush toilets available, a stream nearby, a wood to play in and investigate. Where? Devon, Cornwall or North Wales? No, surprisingly just five miles away from Marsh Hill Junior and Infant School, Erdington, in the heart of the West Midland conurbation. In fact at Streetly, just a stone's throw from Chester Road, but beautifully shielded from the road by that lovely little wood, so that the actual site gives the appearance of being quite secluded and is amazingly quiet.

He went on to describe a camping adventure designed as the catalyst in the middle of an environmental studies project for third-year juniors. This was the first taste of being away from home for many of the seventy ten-year olds who took part at the cost of £1 per child.

The point being made is that children can be introduced to the experience of camping without the necessity of going a long way from home. One can be adventurous in ideas and methods without having to be either an explorer in the wilderness or a seasoned long-distance traveller. Perhaps, as in most things, it is best to gain experience of camp life slowly and over a long period of time rather than by rushing to try and do everything all at once. This is particularly sound advice when other people's children are involved in the experiment!

If the camping bug bites the children, then the fun and thrill will remain with them for much of the rest of their lives.

**Camping method**

There's nothing quite like living under canvas. Nigel Hunt (1969) described it vividly when he wrote:

> The first tent is a space capsule (and you can seem as vulnerable if you are nervous of camping). Your orbit into moon mists and sun haze, running scent and blowing grass may seem too close to nature for comfort. Until you try it. And until you use the astronaut's method of living encapsulated in a new dimension. Yes, *method*: this is your answer to any fears of catching cold, getting wet or being besieged by insects, animals and gales.
>
> It is method which ranges from living inside your sleeping bag in a small mountain tent in bad weather to sleeping in the living space of your big frame tent as an after-dinner nap.

If you follow his methodology you will see how communing with the forces of nature is made more comfortable by knowledge and scientific understanding. There is no need to become a troglodite just because you decide to enter the world of nature. But, with understanding, you are better prepared to live in harmony with the environment.

Teachers who have never camped but who feel that the outdoor life is for them and their children would do well to study Hunt's book in its entirety. There are several other useful books available which put the experience of veterans down simply for the uninitiated, but there is no substitute to going off for a weekend to try it for yourself. Remember the golden rule 'Teacher does it first', then take the initiative.

In chapter 11, entitled 'Camp Life', of his book, Eric Hemery (1970) gives a first-class summary which is helpful for all people contemplating camping, whether they have done it before or not. It is a useful resource book for a teacher who seeks to brush up his knowledge. Above all Hemery makes it quite clear that camping is not a hit and miss affair – if done properly. There are the rules to the game and a complete range of techniques to be learnt in perfecting the art. In lyrical terms, camping expertise is the 'key to the gateway of the kingdom of nature' – and 'fools must not rush in where angels fear to tread'.

**Some practicalities**

Teachers have become accustomed to using their initiative. No school can afford to buy every item of equipment it needs and it is necessary for staff to perfect the gentle art of scrounging, whether it be in the acquisition of material things or just ideas.

Camping, above all else, depends upon careful preparation. One can get by with a minimum on a two-man hiking expedition; but when forty or more children are involved, decisions have to be made well in advance and certain plans must be firmly implemented. Buying food in a small Welsh holiday resort is far more expensive than in a large city 'cash and carry' wholesalers. Register your camping club with someone who supplies catering establishments, then go along well in advance of the camp's start and purchase the bulk of your supplies. In the Marsh Hill and Yenton venture which was referred to earlier, the quartermaster, Vic Watson, planned all the menus in advance and worked out the quantity of each commodity. Each year the basic menu holds good, although it will be adjusted annually according to supply and demand and the children's response to the meals. There will always be someone who doesn't like something. It's quite amazing how fussy some children can be and pretty obvious that taking them away from home is going to do their digestive system a power of good. They either eat or starve, and after a day or so in the fellowship of the camp every sort of child decides on the former. What's more, with gentle persuasion from the leaders, they grow up and enjoy themselves.

Catering tins of vegetables and large cartons of cornflakes and sacks of sugar or potatoes are very heavy. Ideally these should be brought from the suppliers and stored in school. Put them somewhere safe, bearing in mind you don't want to move them again until you load up for the journey. Of course, if you could load them straight into a van and leave them there overnight before you set out that would be ideal, but perhaps that's too much of a pipe-dream. When you get to camp, one tent should be set aside as the 'grub tent' and entry to that should be closely restricted to the cook and his or her helpers. By the way, don't forget to take a tin opener. The tins can be stacked in two groups – vegetables and meats on one side and jams, fruits, sweets on the other. It will be necessary for a periodic check to be made on what quantities are left and one may decide to replenish the larder where deficiencies are obvious. In the Talybont camps the milkman, the baker and the butcher visited the site daily, so perishable food was not much of a problem. Experience has shown that it is a good economy to buy sweets and lollipops from the 'cash and carry'. These can be taken to camp and sold once or twice a day in the tuck shop – that's a duty for one member of staff. If you want the camp to keep a good reputation, don't sell chewing gum.

Perhaps the best guide to food quantities and menus is to read through the details given below. They are from the camping notebook of Vic Watson and they have proved more than adequate over several expeditions. (The high cost of potatoes at the time of writing may prevail and, if so, it may be considered wise to seek an alternative, but do remember that 'spud bashing' is an integral part of camp life!)

*Friday evening (or day of arrival)*
Own stew from two catering-size stewed beef tins; potatoes, carrots, peas; tinned fruit and cream

| | | |
|---|---|---|
| *Saturday* | Breakfast: | Cornflakes, bacon, scrambled egg, beans, fried potatoes |
| | Dinner: | Sandwiches |
| | Evening meal: | Faggots, peas, potatoes; steamed pudding and custard |
| | | (Every day the midday meal is composed of sandwiches, crisps, fruit and a drink of orange or lemon squash.) |
| *Sunday* | Breakfast: | Cornflakes, bacon, scrambled egg, fried potatoes and tomatoes |

| *Sunday* | Evening meal: | Ham, baked beans, potatoes; plums and custard |
|---|---|---|
| *Monday* | Breakfast: | Cornflakes, bacon, scrambled egg, fried potatoes, fried bread and tomatoes |
| | Evening meal: | Sausage, peas, carrots, potatoes; swiss roll and custard |
| *Tuesday* | Breakfast: | Cornflakes, bacon/sausage, beans, tomatoes |
| | Evening meal: | Stew; steamed pudding and custard |
| *Wednesday* | Breakfast: | Cornflakes, bacon, scrambled egg and beans |
| | Evening meal: | Fried ham, carrots, peas and potatoes; fruit and jelly |
| *Thursday* | Breakfast: | Cornflakes, fried egg, fried potatoes, beans and tomatoes |
| | Evening meal: | Sausage, peas, carrots, potatoes; red plums, sliced peaches and custard |
| *Friday* | Breakfast: | Cornflakes, fried potatoes, fried bread, scrambled egg, tomatoes |
| | Evening meal: | Faggots, baked beans, potatoes; rice pudding and red plums |
| *Saturday* | Breakfast: | Cornflakes, bacon, egg, baked beans |
| | Evening meal: | Stew; pineapple, cream, custard |
| *Sunday* | Breakfast: | Cornflakes, bacon, egg, fried potatoes |
| | Evening meal: | Cold meat, carrots, peas, potatoes; fruit and custard or fruit in jelly |
| *Monday* | Breakfast: | Cornflakes, fried potatoes, tomatoes, egg |
| | Evening meal: | Faggots, baked beans, potatoes; rice pudding |
| *Tuesday* | Breakfast: | Cornflakes, fried potatoes, fried egg tomatoes and fried bread |
| | Evening meal: | Sausage, beans, peas, carrots, potatoes; custard with any remaining fruit |
| *Wednesday* | Breakfast: | Cornflakes, sausage, eggs, beans |

Lunchtime sandwiches before or during the return journey.

In the morning the fried potatoes are made from cold cooked potatoes from the night before. Cooking is done mainly on Calor Gas rings, though a wood fire is used for large dixies of hot water. These are essential requirements for washing up, cleaning the kitchen and the maintenance of hygiene. The 'bog man' who deals with the toilet arrangements each morning, before many people are up, and later in the day if necessary, will require a hot wash and some water may be necessary for cleaning cuts, abrasions and other minor ailments during sick parade.

GENERAL GUIDE TO AMOUNTS REQUIRED

All the tins mentioned are catering-sized. The following is a rough guide for a camp of sixty people. Readers will doubtless plan their own supplies according to availability of provisions and size of contingent. But this supply pattern has worked very well over several camps.

Potatoes – 28 lbs per day (this allows for breakfast frying). With present costs it could be too expensive in future camps.
Peas or carrots – when used on their own, two tins; together, one of each. (Carrots are not very popular with children; usually we used twice as many beans or peas as carrots: leftovers go into stew.)
Baked beans – popular: on their own, two tins.
Faggots – one each per person: only good if you have a friendly butcher. Catering tins of ravioli are good substitutes.
Sausages – three each per person. Tinned hot dog sausages are better.
Stew – 10 lbs of minced meat. Take a supply of stewed steak.
Mixed vegetables – two tins to go in with stew dishes.
Bacon – 5 lbs per meal. Open a large tin of ham, fry it. Hold some back. Only buy bacon three times in the fortnight.
Eggs – scrambled, one for every two persons: fried – one each.
Milk – 25 pints a day: 15 for breakfast.
Bread – settled at ten loaves a day; Three used at breakfast and the rest were used for sandwiches. Order more than ten on the first day so that there will always be an overlap. Use them in order of delivery.
Fruit – two tins per meal.
Jelly – mixed in large serving tins with fruit. Eight jellies per tin. One tin of fruit cocktail with each tin of jelly.

Rice pudding – large tins are very good.

Gravy – can be made from large tin of powdered soup: half a gallon per meal.

Butter – approximately 3 lbs needed for sandwiches. After the first day we bought 5 lbs of butter every other day. The new soft margarine is very good.

Sugar – used 72 lbs.

Jam – took 1 lb jars for convenience. Recommend twenty-four jars.

Marmalade – six small jars needed.

Steam pudding – eighteen per meal.

Squash – took fifteen one-gallon canisters of orange squash.

Tomatoes – eight catering-size tins. Approximately one per breakfast.

Coffee – two large tins.

Tea – 3 lbs.

Cocoa – five large tins, drinking chocolate better than cocoa. Check the size of tin (its cuppage) when buying.

Ravioli – four large tins.

Cold meat – pork shoulder 10 lb tins. A good buy at about £5–£6.

Evaporated milk – one dozen large tins.

Paste spreads: for lunchtime sandwiches. Difficult to say how many are really required. If too much is taken the unopened residue can be resold on return. Wholesale sold in dozens. Eight dozen may be sufficient.

Cheese spread – couple of packets from wholesaler.

Sauce – one dozen small black: one dozen small tomato.

Cornflakes – two cases of giant size required (about three boxes every breakfast time).

Custard – a bag of caterer's mix that only requires addition of water.

Salt – one large container.

Pepper – very small amount.

Crisps – popular but bulky and difficult to store if damp. We took four boxes with 48 packets per box. These lasted roughly three days. Crisps are a useful addition to midday sandwiches.

SUNDRIES

These included the following: a two-gallon can of cooking oil; a one-gallon can of washing-up liquid which was dispensed from empty squeezy containers; four one-gallon cans of disinfectant; several boxes of matches; dish mops – take a dozen; one large box of paper towels; candles – a dozen; paraffin from the local garage and Jeyes Fluid – two of the one-gallon can size.

Remember the more you can take with you, bought at wholesale price, the less money need be spent at the local shops.

## That minibus

There is some confusion as to the regulations concerning minibuses and the need for a Public Service Vehicle licence. For the last twelve years, the writer has run a Ford Transit twelve-seater instead of a car. It has been rather expensive but it has also been extremely useful with school teams and groups engaged in all sorts of out-of-school activities. But few teachers are prepared for the expense this entails – it is a special sort of dedication. The whole debate ranges around the question of payments. If you are prepared to own such a vehicle privately and not charge for its use, that's OK. But if any payment is made then the regulations make it clear that the vehicle becomes categorized as a PSV – and this may hold good for a private-hire vehicle. Consult the latest regulations on this: nobody wants to find themselves breaking the law with other people's children. Any contribution – even to school funds – which gives a passenger the right to be carried on the vehicle must be regarded in law as 'hire or reward' and this will then define the vehicle as a PSV. Children can travel in a properly insured minibus, provided they do so 'for free'. School-owned vehicles may have to conform to the latest provisions of the Road Traffic Act, which may be altered to bring it into line with the EEC regulations. Adequate insurance is vital for such transport.

## References

HEMERY, E. (1970) *Wilderness Camping in Britain* Robert Hale

HUNT, N. (1969) *Camping* (Illustrated Teach Yourself Series) Brockhampton Press

WATSON, V. R. (1976) 'Camp 1975' in M. J. Arkinstall *et al Environmental Studies – Facing the Problems* Birmingham: Lyndhurst Primary School

Chapter 6

# Study visits

### Different views of study visits
Taking children away from home for a short period of time, be it two days or two weeks, opens up new perspectives in education. The staff and the children share a relationship which is not mere schooling. For a brief moment in their lives the pupils assume a new prestige and a new importance. They are young people who must learn to stand on their own two feet, make their own decisions and face up to life in the real world where there are no school walls to offer them protection and relative isolation. Character is built and the children are socialized into the ways of their society – the biological entity, a child, grows up and achieves physical, emotional and social maturity. Many teachers who have taken their pupils away on study visits to a new environment, be it the seaside, the country or the lonely hills or lakes, would agree that the experience is more than worthwhile. The communal life, beset with different activities and fresh experiences, helps the child to free the apron strings, to understand what life is all about and to learn to live with others in a world where sharing is becoming a matter of sheer survival.

Local authorities have accepted the value of this experiential learning setting by establishing centres for study in the Lake District, the Scottish Highlands, the Welsh hill country, the seaside, the town and the country. Field study courses, once the privilege of geology or biology students, are now being made available to children of all ages and backgrounds. In the corridors of power, money is being set aside to increase the opportunities for 'ordinary' children to go away from home, in school time, often at little or no cost to their parents, so that they might experience the joys of nature, gaze wonderingly at their inheritance and learn to appreciate man's place in the universe.

Awareness is learnt and a critical faculty begins to develop.

Groups of schools have cooperated to provide accommodation, and keen parents have helped to raise money so that their children may be able to learn from a new experience, whether on a farm, in a Nissen hut or aboard a converted longboat. Slowly but surely, study visits are being integrated into the regular school curriculum and it is becoming accepted that they are not just holidays or picnics, but another way of providing a meaningful and challenging situation. There are many different facets to illustrate the theme, all of credit to the dedication of teachers, and the details which follow are intended to show the scope and the value of some of the work which is being done.

Study visits fall into certain categories. There are the closely structured courses where everything in the programme is prearranged and then tackled professionally – rather like a rigorous summer school of the Open University. The object of these courses is to transfer quickly new knowledge and skills to the course members. There may be some specific training purpose involved or some objective such as fieldwork for a geography or biology examination. Most teachers will have experienced this sort of course which is very demanding and very tiring for the recipients. There are also the half and half courses where children go to a new environment and use it as the basis for learning experiences but, at the same time, manage to enjoy a social occasion as they live together away from their parents – possibly for the first time. Then there are the fellowship courses – some teachers like to refer to them as 'holiday rather than work' – but even though the emphasis is on the social experience the children will inevitably learn a great deal incidentally.

As with analysis of the curriculum, most courses have a certain mixture about them. They are inevitably a compromise, somewhere between what one would ideally do and what one can manage in terms of the visible constraints of any situation. One group of schools in Birmingham have a hutted centre a few miles away from the city. Children go there each weekend in groups, but after a couple of visits it becomes increasingly difficult to find a new programme. The scope of the centre is limited. In contrast, other schools go further afield to Campamarinas or Holiday Weekend Centres where the children enjoy a whole new range of activities such as pony trekking, speedboat racing, shooting, fishing or canoeing, and life suddenly assumes all sorts of new possibilities. Money and time are the only limitations on the *dolce vita*. But whatever the course may be, it will fail miserably without the right sort of teachers. They need tolerance, patience, dedication and a very large share of energy.

All the usual preliminaries apply to study visits. The teacher should go to the centre first. He or she should know what facilities exist and what the probable difficulties might be. A programme should be planned, if only in outline form, and if there is a warden or head of centre he or she should be brought into the act. In this connection it is far better to go and talk to the appropriate person than to send a constant stream of letters with queries and problems. Medical and legal preparations must be dealt with and the parents should be given some outline of what is planned, together with some time scale so that they know roughly when their children will return. There should be an emergency system of communications set up and a special telephone number so that contact can be made, in emergency only, either way between the visitors and those still at home.

In spite of what various regulations might say to the contrary, there needs to be a good proportion of staff. The more adults there are, the better will be the possibilities for teaching and learning and the easier will be the burden of control and responsibility. One must not rule out the chance that one of the staff might be ill during the trip and that the others must be able to cope effectively and without too much of a strain. Staffing economies may make it harder to take children away from school, but the children's gain in terms of character alone will justify the effort.

Let us suppose that the arrangements can be dealt with satisfactorily. The questions one then asks are where shall we go, and what shall we do? As with most pedagogical issues, the answers vary with the special circumstances of the school party. Look around and find out what is on offer. You may have to book six months or more in advance! Then plan your trip with regard to the particular features of the venue. Try to achieve a balance between work and enjoyment, leisure and involvement, nature and technology, the past and the present, the mediocre and the extraordinary. More will be said about this in chapter 9. Read what others have done, albeit in a different setting, and talk to colleagues in other schools. Every bit of preparation is an investment for your own course. The school's resource centre or staff library should house worksheets, advertising material and notes on trips and courses. These are a valuable guide and when your trip is over, writing it up will help others to plan their excursions into the unknown. The notes which follow are descriptions of what teachers have done. They might give useful pointers for your study course.

## A middle school exchange visit

The details given are descriptive of an exchange visit planned between two middle schools – one in the West Midlands and the other in the South of England. These are described more fully in *Environmental Studies – Facing the Problems* (Arkinstall *et al* 1976) on the theme of putting environmental studies into practice. Tony Wainwright, at that time headteacher at St Joseph's School in Sutton Coldfield, arranged for two members of staff from Park Mead Middle School in Cranleigh to spend a weekend with him to discuss the necessary arrangements for the exchange. Forty Sutton children would stay in Cranleigh and forty children from Park Mead would visit Sutton Coldfield. The actual events would take place in March and in May, and a full programme would be arranged for both expeditions.

Both education authorities gave their permission and the plans were set in motion. Perhaps it is best to let Tony Wainwright take up the story.

'Obviously such an enterprise needed a clear set of aims and objectives. The organizers could initially see a tremendous social value in the exercise. Few of these children had previously been away from their parents other than on organized journeys through school, Scouts or Guides, where their friends were with them all the time. On this occasion it was to be a case of staying in a home for a week with a family they had never met before. A very careful matching procedure was essential. St Josephs, being the smaller school, started the machinery moving and parents of children in the eleven to twelve age group were notified of the proposed exchange. There were forty replies in the affirmative: twenty-three girls and seventeen boys. These children were asked to fill in a questionnaire stating details of numbers in their family, pets, hobbies and interests and their likes and dislikes. The staff then added further details regarding the personality of the child and giving some indication of academic ability and any other information that seemed relevant in helping towards a successful match. These questionnaires were then sent to Park Mead where the teachers set out to provide suitable partners from the hundred children who had asked to be considered. Forty were duly selected and the remaining sixty were promised a place on other journeys being organized by the school that year.

'The pairings were ready at the beginning of the spring term and letters were exchanged between the children. In some cases, parents had telephoned the parents of their child's partner and contact had already been established. This was important, as children suffer from minor allergies which might not be known at school. One child, for instance, was allergic to feather pillows and another to nylon sheets.

'Letters were sent in January to both sets of parents outlining the details of requirements for the visit. Insurance arrangements were verified and the journey was costed, the major item of expenditure being for a forty-five seater coach for the week. Both schools accepted the most reasonable figure after checking that the coach was of a high quality. This figure, together with insurance costs, proposed admission charges and various other small items, enabled both schools to cost the exchange at £10 per child. This proved to be a slight overestimate and all the children later received a refund. A maximum figure of £3 was set for pocket money, which was to include buying presents for the family. As an exercise in economics, the children were to look after the money themselves and it was their responsibility to make it last the week.

'Whilst the pastoral preparations with their obvious social benefits were taking place, the organizers were busy planning the academic part of the exercise. It was decided that, as they were on the spot, the teachers from each school would plan the others' working week. The Park Mead teachers expressed a desire for the theme for the week to be the Industrial Revolution. The St Joseph's staff were less specific and agreed to undertake an interesting range of visits and experiences with an historical bias whilst in the South. All the staff were aware of the possibility of homesickness amongst the children and it was decided to provide a comprehensive itinerary involving plenty of work for the children. Questionnaires were composed for most visits. Opportunities for creative writing were presented and encouraged and detailed diaries were kept in preparation for follow-up work and an exhibition on return to their own schools. The social needs of the children were to be catered for in organized games sessions, and a grand finale in the form of a disco. The final stages of the preparation involved the compilation of registration lists with addresses and telephone numbers of all the children from both schools.'

The author then goes on to describe the visits in detail and the programme of activities. It is obvious that this was not a holiday trip. On the first day of their visit to the Midlands the Park Mead children visited Rugeley Power Station in the morning. Here they saw a film on electricity and experienced a guided tour of the station, answering the multi-choice questions on their worksheets. In the afternoon, after a packed lunch, they visited the Mines Rescue Station at Hednesford and after a question and answer session with the station staff they were taken into a simulated mine to see, at first hand, conditions at the coal face. Their day ended with a choice of indoor games, outdoor games or swimming back at St Joseph's. Tiredness was deemed to be a good way of preventing homesickness. The second day was set aside for the trip to Ironbridge and Coalbrookdale. After the morning in the Ironbridge Gorge Museum where the guide patiently answered all their questions, the children spent their afternoon in the Blists Hill open air museum with a visit to the Tar Tunnel. They saw at first hand the Hay Inclined Plane which was used to raise tub boats between the Shropshire Canal and the Coalport Basin. On their return to school there were yet more games – the children chose different activities to those they had selected the day before.

'The itinerary for Wednesday followed a different pattern. The visiting children and their hosts were given the morning off to relax. The opportunity was there for an extra hour in bed for those who were tired, yet most children went into town with their host-parents and did some shopping. After lunch they assembled at school for the coach to take them to Gas Street Basin. Here they visited the museum on canal history for a short talk and answered some questions on their worksheets. During the afternoon they went on a boat trip along the canal to Spon Lane Locks. The questionnaire kept them busy on the outward journey through the old industrial areas of Birmingham. The return trip was more of a social event and the children sang and enjoyed themselves. They arrived back at school in the early evening when they were met and taken home.

'A day in Matlock was arranged for Thursday and the children learnt of the ancient processes for producing iron in that part of the country. They also saw much of the beautiful countryside in that part of Derbyshire. Once again the afternoon return was after school closure and arrangements had been made for the children to be met. The Science Museum was on the agenda for

Friday morning. A task sheet was given to the children and they were asked to list and understand the function of many of the exhibits. This proved to be a very interesting morning and much of what they saw linked in with other things observed during the week. Lunches were eaten in the gardens by the Repertory Theatre, appropriately beneath the gaze of the statue of Boulton, Watt and Murdoch. The children returned to St Joseph's to spend the afternoon in school with their partners. They returned home for tea and reassembled in school later in the evening for a disco and a short pantomime entertainment given by the staff.'

Doubtless they returned home with many interesting stories to tell of their stay in the Midlands. But what of the Sutton children when they made a reciprocal visit in May? They had the advantage of having met their friends already, so much of the shyness had disappeared. Their programme was just as strenuous and it is important to summarize it. The phrase 'fieldwork' is beginning to mean something.

'A lengthy journey to Portsmouth was on the agenda for Monday and the children were asked to observe the placenames and particularly the public house signs *en route*. Many of these had a distinctly nautical flavour. On their arrival in Portsmouth, the children were taken on a conducted tour of HMS *Victory*. This was particularly interesting and the guide, a young marine, painted a realistic picture of conditions for sailors in Nelson's time. After lunch on the beach, the children travelled to and from the Isle of Wight by hovercraft.'

Tuesday was set aside for relaxation and on Wednesday the morning visit was to the Natural History Museum at Haslemere. After working on some questionnaires the children visited the Punchbowl Nature Trail at Hindhead before they returned to their adoptive school. The longest trip was reserved for Thursday. This was to Brighton for a visit to the Dolphinarium in the morning and the Royal Pavilion later in the day where the children learnt of the extravagance of the Prince Regent.

'The final full day was taken up by two visits. The morning journey was to the Roman Palace at Fishbourne. This aroused the interest of the children, who were most impressed with the reconstruction work of the archaeologists. They then spent the afternoon at the Singleton Open Air Museum. This really brought to life the ways of the Middle Ages and there was so much to see and take in that the organizers thought it worth a full day's visit on a later occasion. The high spot of the afternoon was provided by a volunteer blacksmith when he made an axe head for the children. All of them returned to school very tired and excited after a week of many experiences.'

## A study centre in Oxford

The exchange visit was very adventurous and entailed twice the normal amount of planning, as both parties had to be catered for. But it is very significant that the whole group were kept together – at least as far as visits were concerned. When a class of children from Lyndhurst Primary School spent a school week in Oxford the programme was arranged to keep the groups small and manageable and the staff bore the brunt of the work.

The children's working day was planned around one main activity which lasted from soon after breakfast until tea time. The evening was then given over to classroom sessions, games and other entertainments. On the first and last days all the children were kept together to share a visit to a local school and a swim in their pool and to walk over the hills and play wide games. The recipe proved successful, if strenuous, and it is detailed below for those who might consider a similar organization of learning time. Tuesday, Wednesday and Thursday were treated as the same and the programme of work designed for each group would be repeated – although there would be variations according to the children's needs and responses – so that each of the twenty-eight children covered the same range of activities during the seventy-two-hour span.

The children were organized into three groups – two nines and a ten. These were referred to as groups A, B and C. The group selection was arbitrary, but there were boys and girls in each group. The staff took each of the three groups on successive days on their planned activities which covered the whole spectrum of change, location and structure – the bases for the Schools Council Environmental Studies approach. The immediate environs were used as a starting point for observation and analysis. To facilitate the work, lunches were taken in picnic form and the whole class came together at tea time, when they quickly exchanged news and views of the day's happenings. The basic programme was as follows:

*Group A*
This group conducted an urban study of Headington. They used printed sheets and clipboards and collected information on

F

shopping habits, the use of the park and the busy traffic scene. They met local people who, incidentally, informed their teachers that they thought the children were polite and a credit to their school and they surveyed the church and the quarry area in their quest for knowledge. Their equipment included a noisemeter, a Kodak Instamatic and a Polaroid camera. Their one advantage was that they were near enough to the study centre to return before tea time and, in many respects, their data could be stored for later use in making comparisons between areas. It is interesting to recall one discovery: the great writer and Professor of English, C. S. Lewis, was buried in a local church and the children were fascinated by his memorial.

*Group B*
The members of this group learnt a great deal about man's insignificance compared to nature, for they experienced an orienteering exercise which took them well into the country and away from the usual urban environment. A certain amount of preliminary work was done in the classroom to make this possible. It was necessary to revise grid references and refresh the memory on map colours, signs and symbols; many of the children had never used a compass before and they benefited greatly from the experience and practice involved. Each child had a schedule of work which included finding some answers from direct intensive observations made *en route* and by trying out two new techniques – taking a soil sample and drawing a simple sketch map. The whole exercise was very exciting and the children enjoyed it immensely. On one of the three days it was so hot that a detour had to be made from the original route and the minibus was diverted after tea time to pick up a dozen very tired campaigners.

*Group C*
This group's activities might be looked upon as the most flamboyant and, perhaps, the least energetic. By use of the minibus the group of children was transported a distance of ten miles or so to the old town of Woodstock. After a quick walk round with the chance to send a postcard home to Mum they visited the museum where they received the red-carpet treatment. A guided tour by a member of the staff was the prelude to a lesson in one of the craft rooms. Two groups studied the blacksmith's shop and the third learnt of the difficulties the housewife had to

endure in the days before automation and technology. The museum provided excellent worksheets and it was a tired and hungry group which sat down each day by the artificial lake at Blenheim Palace to enjoy their prepacked lunch. But children soon return to full speed. Lunch over, a quick antilitter patrol and they were ready for all the palace had to offer. Many of them will remember the fine porcelain, the rich tapestries depicting battle scenes in a bygone age, the Winston Churchill display and that intricate lock on the door, produced by a Birmingham firm of locksmiths. What a rich feast of culture. After leaving the magnificent library and chapel to emerge into the summer sunshine and seek those necessary lollies and ice cream there was a trip on the lake, a walk up to the monument and, for some, a return diversion to the quiet country church at Bladon to stand for a moment at the graveside of Churchill's last resting place. History began to come alive.

So, by switching the groups daily, but not the activities, each child was able to experience all three schemes of work – though the staff, like true professionals, only worked in one area.

It is easy to criticize, especially in retrospect, but perhaps the planned programme was too adventurous. Certainly it left little time for consolidation. But as this was the first study venture for that particular school it was an attempt to taste the flavour of fieldwork and to see how quite young children could cope with lessons that were more than a little different.

Social experience was not overlooked either. There were evening activities as well as the work. On one occasion a local inhabitant came to talk to the children about the doctor who had once owned the centre. On two nights there were visits to the nearby swimming baths. A camp fire had been planned, but the weather was so fine that a treasure hunt was arranged instead. Sometimes a spontaneous activity like that just captures the children's imagination, especially where there is a competitive element like finding the treasure first. There were the usual games of rounders, football and cricket. Few children seemed to be lacking in energy or enthusiasm, even after a nonstop twelve-hour day.

Nothing has been said about the domestic chores and the arrangements for meals. In this particular trip that was all taken care of by the domestic bursar and her staff. The study centre is run by the education authority and all the teacher has to be concerned with is the health and education of the children. Apart from table laying and washing up there was very little left for the youngsters to do, although they were expected to keep their dormitories clean and respectable. In assessing the value of this sort of study visit one should not forget two things. First of all, a new area provides a new environment with all its many possibilities for discovery and opportunities to practise new skills – map reading, traffic surveys, data collection, photography. Secondly, it provides the social setting for a group of children and adults to live together. Many children mature visibly during such an experience and return home more appreciative and aware of the sweetness of life. Self reliance and confidence are by-products of a successful study trip. It really is a pity that such expeditions cannot be made a regular and obligatory part of the curriculum and that, in some instances, financial limitations may prevent the most needy children from going away from home for a short time.

Where you go and what you do are not quite as important as the fact that you do go. Such experiences are truly educative ones and have their own intrinsic value. The children's enthusiasm will prove this to any critic.

**The Isle of Man experience**
Court Farm Primary School's spring bank holiday was spent in the Isle of Man and the details which follow are an example of another approach to the study trip. The headteacher, Brian Smith, describes it as an educational holiday. His notes are reproduced almost in their entirety.

'It was at 06.45 hours on Friday, 28 May, that parents and children met outside school for the beginning of their journey along the M6 to Liverpool and thence across the Irish Sea to Douglas in the Isle of Man for their educational holiday.

'Why the Isle of Man, you might ask? Why an educational holiday at all? Well, there are certain advantages to staying within the British Isles. It is less expensive, there is less travelling to get there and our children do benefit from spending a few days with their friends, freed from the usual parental influences. They learn to live together in harmony and adjust and organize themselves to their new environment.

'The 28 May might have been the first day of the visit but the planning had begun back in the previous September when five members of staff had agreed to go away for a week. Four of them knew what would be expected and the fifth one would soon find out. The Isle of Man had been chosen on account of its accessibility. It is a self-contained unit; it has a very interesting history and it offers both staff and children a variety of scenery and entertainment. Finding suitable accommodation proved to be a problem without using a travel agent but, after several letters and telephone calls, a hotel in Douglas seemed to be ideal. In choosing this hotel, factors such as position, size, bedrooms, food and prices were uppermost in mind but, if possible, one should always check personally for cleanliness, fire precautions, toilet and washing facilities. Having settled the actual accommodation, the costings were made by consulting the Isle of Man Steam Packet Company and coach firms both at home and on the island. A charge of £30 each was agreed upon, a meeting of interested parents was arranged and we felt as if we were on our way, even though it was still September. Paying-in cards were issued, deposits banked, and weekly payments were encouraged – the parents having been informed that money accrued would gain interest.

'A programme of work was arranged for the children who would be going and this was carried out alongside the preparations. All the children were taught about the journey (time, distance, speeds and directions); the places they would visit during the trip; the history of the island and its particular relationship with the British Isles. Details were stored in scrapbooks which included maps, diagrams, writing and pictures acquired from brochures. The Isle of Man Tourist Board proved very helpful at this stage, providing posters, leaflets, travel guides and three 16 mm cine films which were shown to children and parents.

'Eventually the great day arrived. Had we forgotten anything? The consent forms had been signed, insurance arranged; all the children had been medically examined by the school nurse; all the addresses and telephone numbers and booklets had been distributed, and rooms in the hotel allocated. If anything had been forgotten it was now too late. It remained only to sit back and enjoy the holiday — the children did.

*Friday*
'The journey was uneventful for the staff but very exciting for the children, the smallest of whom seemed to have the largest and heaviest suitcases. The only discordant note was struck when, halfway along the M6, one child asked when we would be going

through London – after all that work and all those maps we looked at. The boat journey was interesting in more ways than one – now I know that it is possible for children to walk to the Isle of Man! It was pleasing to see how interested they were in the boat, the buildings we had left behind in Liverpool and the outline of the island as it came slowly into view. I wondered what the children had really imagined the boat would be like. Most of them commented on its size and I am convinced that some of them thought we would be rowing across the Irish Sea.

'Four hours on the *Ben-my-Chree* was long enough for all of us, but on reaching Douglas we were soon whisked off to our hotel – an apprehensive moment. My fears were soon dispelled. We were made very welcome and within the hour the children had unpacked, washed, changed their clothes two or three times, explored the hotel and were ready to go further afield. It was going to be a strenuous week. Fortunately we were only minutes away from a large park which was an ideal place for the children to run around in before we returned to the hotel for the evening meal. It was after this that the most thrilling moment took place. We walked down to the beach to see all the children drawn, as if by an unseen force, towards the sea. All the months of preparation had been worthwhile: this was why we were in the Isle of Man.

'And so to bed. Would the children sleep at all? Would the staff get the chance to sleep? We were fortunate, for by midnight all was quiet – apart from a few mature snores and grunts audible in a certain room.

*Saturday*
'Six thirty in the morning is not the best time to get out of bed, but sometimes it is necessary in order to quell disturbances before resuming interrupted dreams. The children were very good and although most of them had washed and dressed by that time they were reasonably quiet. After breakfast, rooms were tidied, pocket money distributed and we were off to explore Douglas. On the beach and along the shore we sampled the atmosphere and saw the electric trains and the horse-drawn trams, and the children were soon tired. After lunch we boarded the coach for our first trip round the island – this time to Peel to visit the castle and to stop *en route* at St Johns to inspect Tynwald Hill, home of the Manx open-air Parliament. Now the children could see their lessons at school coming to life as they imagined the Viking

attacks on the island. The evening was spent in the park and after a game of rounders it was certain members of staff who were the most tired.

### Sunday
'This was to have been one of our most enjoyable days for we had planned a visit by electric train to Laxey where we would meet 'Lady Isabella' (a giant waterwheel), spend some time on the beach and in the Laxey Glen Gardens. But it rained very heavily. We were impressed by the wheel, but we were soon so wet that after eating our sandwiches we had to return to the hotel to dry out. After all that it was cards and games in an overcrowded lounge, although some children did venture out later on.

### Monday
'This was one 'free day' in that nothing had been planned. It turned out to be one of the most enjoyable and proved that trips are not always necessary. In the morning one group travelled by electric train to Groundle where they walked through a delightful glen before spending an hour or so on the beach. After lunch back at the hotel they walked round to Douglas Head, saw a collier unloading its cargo and visited the lighthouse where the Scottish keeper was very helpful and informative. The other group spent the morning at the lighthouse and the afternoon at Groundle. Once again, the park proved to be popular for the evening entertainment with its putting green, swings and roundabouts, whilst the big favourite was that game of rounders.

### Tuesday
'A day trip to Port Erin in the south of the island had been arranged, travelling by coach and Victorian steam railway, although only seven miles of this track remains open. This was a most enjoyable day, for the weather was good. We all visited the Railway Museum and the Marine Biological Station and Aquarium, whilst some children walked round the headland to Bradda Head and others walked southwards to the Cragneish open-air Folk Museum.

In the evening we were lucky enough to see some of the TT practices. We had discovered that the start/finish line was quite near to our park and we were able to sit in the grandstand and watch motorcycles flash by at speeds of up to 150 mph. I think it was just about at this time that I had the feeling that I might be short of five teachers at school the following week.

*Wednesday*
'Another day trip. This time to Ramsey in the north. The coach took us through some delightful scenery of hills and valleys, close to Snaefell and along part of the TT course. It was a beautiful day and we all hoped Snaefell would be as clear on Thursday. Ramsey proved to be a real favourite with the children, for we spent the morning in the huge Mooragh Park and the afternoon on the beach. Sandy beaches were not proving popular any more, but the children were finding the rock pools, shells, seaweed and pebbles quite fascinating. In the evening we again saw some of the TT practices – motor cycles and side cars – and a near perfect day ended with another session in the park.

*Thursday*
'Shopping. The children had been allocated pocket money each morning and although some presents had been purchased on our travels during the week, this was the morning set aside for the buying of presents and souvenirs. Off we set. Six children and a teacher were in each group and by eleven o'clock it was all done. The children were able to visit the Manx Cattery or the Museum or stay on the beach.

The afternoon was spent in Castletown, on the beach and in the beautifully preserved Castle Rushen. This is always worth a visit and it is made more enjoyable by the Curator and his wife escorting the children round the castle and speaking to them in the Manx language. In the evening it was the ascent of Snaefell. The coach took us to the bungalow and from there we took the steep pathway to the top. We all made it and our efforts were well rewarded by the magnificent view. The whole of the island was spread out before us and, in the far distance, we could pick out the coastlines of Scotland, Ireland and England. A fitting climax to our week in the Isle of Man.'

The children returned home on Friday. They were tired, happy and glad to be back from an enjoyable holiday. Certain points emerge from the head's account:

1    One teacher to six children is an ideal staffing ratio. Each teacher can be responsible for certain rooms and children's

pocket money and an evening off duty can sometimes be arranged for the staff.

2    On returning to school there is the chance to talk to the children and to find out what they thought about the journey.

3    Questions, photographs, scrap-books and other items can be shared. Slides can be used to show parents. This is one way of making a holiday last ten months and it builds up enthusiasm for going somewhere again next year.

**Reference**
ARKINSTALL, M. J. *et al* (1976) *Environmental Studies – Facing the Problems* Birmingham: Lyndhurst Primary School

# Chapter 7

# The European Community

The Channel Tunnel project seems as far away from reality as ever, yet Concorde has been designed, produced, tested and put into regular service by the airways. The bandwagon of teaching foreign languages in British primary schools has been relegated in favour of teaching the mother tongue. The once mighty pound sterling has yielded its importance before the growing prestige of the mark and the franc. The European Parliament is struggling to assert its power over wayward nation states. We are living in a world of change, a world where, we are told, Europe will only survive in the rat race by cooperative and determined effort. Yet, in spite of this, it is still the exception rather than the rule for children to cross the Channel into Europe and experience the way of life of our Western allies. In terms of politics and economics we are, to some degree, part of the Community but our only claim to cultural identity is in the realm of football. There are, therefore, very good motives for taking our children into Europe. By so doing we can generate understanding, promote friendship and protect the peace.

It is important to bear in mind the fact that restrictions and legal regulations make journeys in Europe just that much harder to organize. For those who are inexperienced and yet want to be more adventurous with their journeys it is a wise move to start off with one of the many tours which are arranged by a school travel agent. The press and educational publications are usually full of advertisements and there is little difficulty in finding out who these agents are and what sort of trip they will arrange for you. In fact, most headteachers find unsolicited pamphlets, offers and prospectus booklets arriving week by week in the school mail. One could criticize these commercial tours – the itinerary is laid down with little room for maneuvre, they are predictable, they arrange visits to the same old places – but there can be no doubt of their popularity and they do make it possible for pupils to experience different aspects of the culture and life style of the country that is being visited. What's more, from the teacher's point of view, they make trips into Europe relatively easy to organize, and one can be reasonably sure of success. On two trips to Belgium, in two successive years, the author found that there was still plenty to see and plenty of scope for inventiveness and originality within the structure of the prearranged timetable. Language barriers are no problem for, to their credit, the people of Europe seem more than competent in speaking English – especially when it helps money to change hands!

## Passport worries

The Passport Office issues comprehensive notes for the guidance of teachers who are making application for a collective passport. These documents are used in place of individual passports for groups of children going abroad under the supervision of a responsible leader. The collective passports only include persons who have not yet reached the age of eighteen and are available for groups of not less than five, nor more than fifty, persons. The leader, who must be over twenty-one, must hold a valid individual passport in his or her own name – a visitor's passport is not acceptable.

The collective passport costs (at present) £8 and application must be made to one of the appropriate passport offices which are listed below. Every member of the party aged sixteen years or over on the date of re-entry into the British Isles must carry a personal identity card, bearing a photograph, during the visit abroad. These cards are available from the Passport Office for completion. Photographs must be securely gummed to the cards and should be certified by a headteacher for school parties and by a person of similar standing, but not the leader of the party, in other cases. The application form (Passport Office 1972) states:

Completed identity cards, where required, must be forwarded to the Passport Office with the application for a collective passport. The cards are only accepted by the various foreign authorities when officially endorsed. The number and date of issue of the collective passport should not be inserted on the cards by the leader; they will be added by the Passport Office.

AREA PASSPORT OFFICES
For Scotland and Northern Ireland
*Glasgow* Passport Office, 1st floor, Empire House, 131 West Nile Street, Glasgow G1 2RY

For Cheshire, Cleveland, Clwyd, Cumbria, Derbyshire, Durham, Greater Manchester, Gwynedd, Humberside, Lancashire, Merseyside, Northumberland, North Yorkshire, Nottinghamshire, South Yorkshire, Staffordshire, Tyne and Wear, West Yorkshire
*Liverpool* Passport Office, 5th floor, India Buildings, Water Street, Liverpool L2 0QZ

For Greater London, Middlesex
*London* Passport Office, Clive House, 70 Petty France, London SW1H 9HD

For Avon, Berkshire, Cornwall, Devon, Dorset, Dyfed, East Sussex, Gloucestershire, Gwent, Hampshire, Hereford and Worcester, Isle of Wight, Mid Glamorgan, Oxfordshire, Powys, Salop, Somerset, South Glamorgan, Surrey (less London Boroughs), West Glamorgan, West Sussex, Wiltshire
*Newport* Passport Office, Olympia House, Upper Dock Street, Newport, Gwent NPT 1XA

For Bedfordshire, Buckinghamshire, Cambridgeshire, Essex (less London Boroughs), Hertfordshire (less London Boroughs), Leicestershire, Lincolnshire, Norfolk, Northamptonshire, Suffolk, Warwickshire, West Midlands
*Peterborough* Passport Office, 55 Westfield Road, Peterborough PE3 6TG

Do check for visa requirements of foreign authorities.


**Insurance and indemnity**
As has been said before, different educational authorities have their own interpretations and regulations with regard to insuring children and staff for journeys abroad. One of the first things a planner should do is to look into this and establish what his or her authority demands. The Birmingham Education Committee has a section in its *Notes For Guidance* which deals expressly with

educational visits and special mention is made of visits to foreign countries.

It is made quite clear that 'adequate insurance cover' must be obtained well before the trip takes place and insurance cover of 'the minimum' is to be treated with great suspicion. It might be considered prudent to pay an additional premium to increase the amount of cover available. This cost will be incorporated into the costings of the trip in the normal manner. Parents should be told just what cover is provided so that, if they desire, they could make their own extra provisions.

The European Economic Community regulations on social security cover people on holiday for urgent sickness or accident on the same basis as the insured nationals of their own country. But it is necessary for parents of children who are going abroad to complete form CM1 which may be obtained from any office of the Department of Health and Social Security. When this form has been returned the parents will receive by post form E111 which states that the holder is entitled to medical benefit under the EEC Social Security regulations for the period of their stay in Europe. The scheme for help is fully explained in leaflet SA 28 entitled 'Medical treatment for holiday makers and other temporary visitors to countries of the European Economic Community'. Every organizer of a trip across the Channel should make this leaflet and any other relevant ones part of his stock-in-trade. Perhaps a small section of the staff library or resources centre could be set aside for all such useful documents. The Birmingham Authority emphasizes the importance of insurance in spite of this scheme and places the figure of £1,500 as being the range of the 'minimum cover advisable'.

With directives like this it would be sheer folly not to insure the expedition and most authorities would immediately withhold their official permission.

The writer G. R. Barrell (1975) suggests that the organizer should always have a sizeable float handy to cover an emergency. He points out that even if sufficient insurance cover has been arranged, that of itself will not persuade the local hospital, doctor or undertaker to move into action. Only ready money talks.

It's no good assuring the medical authorities that the members of the party are adequately insured: payment has to be made on the spot, and the insurance issue settled later. A teacher, one of whose pupils has acute appendicitis which needs immediate surgery, is in an impossible position if he cannot find perhaps £100 or more to get the boy admitted to hospital.

Remember the old adage, 'Better to be safe than sorry!'

### Currency restrictions and facilities

It is a worrying affair to have to deal with the exchange of sterling for other currencies. There are certain restrictions in force which vary from time to time and one must find out how current legislation will affect the financial aspect of the school journey. How much money can the visitor take out of the United Kingdom? What is the best way to change English money into the correct currency? Are there any advantages in doing this before you leave or can you change money when you get to your final destination? What happens if there is any money left over? A whole host of questions bedevil the planner. But they cannot be left to chance or the trip will soon become a disaster.

Perhaps the best piece of advice anyone can have is to find your helpful bank manager and ask him for the form 'Notice to Travellers' which is issued by the Bank of England. Make sure you get the latest edition in case the regulations have changed. The 1973 notice contains some very useful details. It explains the Exchange Control Act of 1947 and emphasizes the dangers of dealing with anybody other than a reputable bank, tour operator or travel agent. Breaking this law can lead to very serious consequences. The world is divided up into the Scheduled Territories and the countries outside these territories where, at the time of writing, you are allowed to take only the equivalent of £300 per journey. This allowance may be taken in several different forms as foreign currency, travellers' cheques or letters of credit and is purely a personal allowance which cannot be used for investment or any other purpose. There are restrictions on the export of British banknotes and postal orders, and trying to take more than the permitted amount out of this country is a customs offence – the same as trying to bring in that extra bottle of whisky or banana brandy. It is also important to know that under the terms of the law as it exists any unused currency which you bring back must be changed back into sterling within a month of your return. This book is not the place for details – do get that 'Notice to Travellers' and find out for yourself.

It is worth reproducing one or two paragraphs from the official booklet, as they are germaine to the present discussion. Part Two has the following hints to offer.

### 28 *Insurance*

All travellers abroad run risks. Unexpected expenses may follow some mishap. You are strongly advised to insure against the breakdown of your car if you are motoring abroad, and against illness, theft or loss, injury and death. Suitable policies can be obtained from most travel agencies or insurance companies.

### 31 *Foreign laws*

Pay heed to customs and currency regulations and any restrictions on photography. You should not act as an intermediary by carrying anything on behalf of other persons into or out of another country unless you have made sure that it is not an offence against the local law. Tourist bureaus and foreign consulates in this country can advise you. Remember that activities directed against a foreign state or its political system may incur severe penalties and that in some countries very severe penalties attach to the illegal possession of drugs.

In short, do be extra careful with your homework when you are arranging a trip abroad. You can avoid much of the donkey work by making use of one of the reputable firms which specialize in European holidays for school parties. Their advice and experience may well prevent mistakes and omissions which could be very expensive both in terms of money and unhappiness. When things go wrong at home remedies are relatively easy – but to be in difficulties in a foreign country is a frightening experience.

### Cameras on the ferry

It has become quite commonplace for children to own the latest in cameras, cassette recorders and transistorized radios. A trip to Europe is a wonderful opportunity to take pictures and to make a movie film to show the people who are left at home. But there is one proviso which ought to be emphasized with parents. If a child is going to bring his Polaroid Swinger or Kodak Instamatic then he should have practised using it at home before the day of the trip. There's nothing more annoying for a teacher trying to fight the nausea of a rough crossing than to be besieged by a child who is asking for help in taking a picture, changing a film or wanting to know which button to press. All this should be part of the school-based preparation, so that the child has confidence in his camera's ability before the moment arrives. It might also be a good idea for the children to take spare films with them in their luggage and, in view of what has happened recently, they should exercise discretion in the choice of their photographic subjects, avoiding police stations, barracks, harbours and any official buildings like the plague. The teacher does not want to be mistaken for an espionage agent. Continental prisons are not pleasant.

## Belgium

A recent school journey to Belgium which took place during the Spring Bank Holiday comprised the following itinerary:

Sunday      Meet at school at 0815 hours. Leave school at 0830. Children will need packed lunch and 50p for their motorway stop. They should also have a duffle or carrier bag and a travelling case.
First stop will be at Scratchwood Services; second stop at Medway Services. Arrival at Ramsgate 1500 hours. Depart from Ramsgate on hovercraft for Calais at 1600 hours. Coaches will leave Calais and arrive at Ostend at approximately 1800 hours.

Monday      The morning will be spent at leisure in Ostend. In the afternoon there will be a visit to Bruges with a trip on the canal.

Tuesday     1000 hours leave for Holland.
Drive through Knokke-le-Zoute (millionaire's paradise). Visit the Island of Walcheren and on to Sluis to see a real working windmill.

Wednesday   In the morning visit Meli Park. Return to the hotel for lunch. In the afternoon visit Ghent.

Thursday    Leave hotel at 0900 hours. Take the 1200 ferry from Calais. Arrive back at school at approximately 1900 hours.

The timetable is clear and concise. All the parents had a copy and, like the children, were able to follow the course of events. Certain features stood out. For instance, anyone who has been to Bruges knows about the canal perfume, the lace shop opposite the

Beguinage and that exhausting climb to the top of the Belfry where even the toughest wilt halfway up but have to continue. Knokke, with its palatial homes, and the windmill at Sluis sound fairly straightforward, but what about those embarrassing sex shops which the children will pass on their way to buy clogs, tablecloths and other souvenirs. Meli Park is a Disneyland centre. Sit and listen to the organist and watch the colourful dancing waters; buy some home-made honey from the shop; be careful as you pass the statue of the little man, especially if someone has activated his fountain with a coin; avoid the witches on their broomsticks as they fly past you and don't forget to put your rubbish in the mouth of the laughing litter-man. But above all, don't drink too many glasses of that extra strong beer. Apart from the official itinerary there's a wealth of fun to be gained in spending pocket money, watching the locals and collecting odd items for the scrap-book competition.

'Here is God's Plenty' might be a fair description of the journey through the Benelux Countries, for the children are learning all the time. One fact which stands out is the great linguistic ability of the inhabitants. Whether they be French-speaking or Flemish, all the shopkeepers, drivers, waiters, guides and officials seem to be multilingual and are more than capable of speaking to visitors in Italian, German or English. Belgium is a place which is full of surprises and it is possible to return there again and again and still find something different. There is a certain charm, a mixture of old and new, a combination of trendy elegance and almost medieval practicality. The country relies upon its tourist trade and if the children are well behaved they will be welcome. An enterprising party leader will be able to negotiate special rates for groups of children to visit the fair or to ride bikes along the promenade at Blankenberg and there will be great fun to be had in buying presents from the many shops, but at all times the teacher will need to supervise the children to see that they don't get lost or become involved in any trouble. The best way to do this is to have small groups directly responsible to an adult and to make sure that the adults are the right sort of people who can combine business with pleasure to make sure that the children get the most out of the tour.

Armed police always seem more imposing and should the teacher find himself in dispute with the law he should ask to see the British consulate official. One such episode nearly ruined a trip for a school about five years ago. Some boys were riding a

G

hired tandem through the streets of Blankenberg when they collided with and scratched an impressive looking Mercedes car. The driver sought the police, and the party leader eventually found himself paying up a great deal of money to put the matter right. That meant less money for trips and a great deal of unnecessary upset and trouble for everyone concerned. The same difficulties might apply when a child has an accident. One boy fell off a sea wall and impaled his back on some rusty metal. He was rushed back to the hotel, bandaged in an old sheet, and spent a very uncomfortable night trying to rest on his stomach. The scar is with him now, a permanent reminder of an unthinking moment. Such incidents can wreck the trip for those who are in charge, so the golden rule when abroad is 'Have a code of disciplined behaviour and stick to it'. Silly children soon spoil a trip for everyone, and stupid behaviour such as playing in the hotel lift or hide and seek in each other's bedrooms is to be deplored and ruthlessly wiped out.

Unfortunately, the British standards of cleanliness, when it comes to avoiding litter, need improvement. Run a competition with so many points each inspection time (twice a day) and give a small prize to the best room: this will help to keep the hotel staff happy and improve the tarnished image of the Englishman abroad. But whatever else you do, make sure that nobody ever eats on board a coach or drops litter; otherwise the party could find themselves walking, and that is definitely no joke! Eating habits and priorities may vary from country to country and some children can be very fussy away from 'mum's food', but part of the foreign adventure is trying new dishes and gaining experiences. Teachers should insist that children don't miss meals and, in a diplomatic way, should try to avoid excessive eating between meals. But where there is a special delicacy children should be gently tempted to try it for themselves. Pancakes or waffles with cream and jam can be quite exciting in an open-air restaurant late at night. Drinking the water abroad should be taboo. Children don't mind cleaning their teeth with a glass of lemonade or Coca Cola; to them it's just another part of the excitement. If the children are going to want sweets during their stay abroad (and, let's face it, most children do) they should take them as a part of their luggage. Chocolate is to be avoided in favour of boiled and packet sweets, and some barley-sugar will quite often assuage the pangs of hunger and ward off impending sickness.

Cafés seem to remain open all day in Belgium and the host can nearly always produce what you want, even if it isn't on show. If there are plenty of teachers with the school party it might be possible for one or two to have an hour off occasionally. A short break and a little refreshment away from the children makes every teacher more efficient when back on duty. The same technique holds good with regard to dormitory patrol, dining room duties and all those other necessary irksome tasks which lead to a well-organized and efficient trip, when they are done properly and in the right spirit. But be prepared for good food, different food and nourishing food. Belgium is not the place for slimmers and the gastronomic art is well perfected. It is easy to overeat as the author did when he faced 'sausage and mash, Belgian style' for the very first time.

## Plea for help

Infant teachers have long used the idea of pinning a label to each child when they take them out of school to the seaside or the zoo. It must seem quite funny to the general public to see rows and groups of children wandering about suitably labelled. In planning a trip abroad it is most valuable to give each child a 'Plea for Help' card – this will be printed in three languages and will contain the name of the child, his school and the address and phone number of his hotel. The children should be instructed beforehand that if they ever do get lost they should take that card to the nearest 'sensible-looking adult' and show it to them. On one trip to Belgium the card which had been provided proved to be a godsend. Jacqueline, aged ten, wrote as follows:

We were in Bruges for the afternoon and Mr Arkinstall and Mr King offered to take us up to the top of the Belfry. The majority went, but a few of us wandered off and found a fair and then it happened!

I momentarily turned round to watch a side show and when I turned back there was absolutely no sign of anyone I knew. So, desperately I took my plea for help card and showed it to a lady who ushered me into a bar, told one of the people in charge and phoned the police.

The police arrived and were going to take me back to the Hotel Astrid but frantically I explained that if they took me back, the others wouldn't know where I was.

Luckily, just at that moment, Mrs Cross spotted me in the police van and my nightmare was over.

Can anyone afford not to prepare these simple cards?

## Worksheets and records

Mention has been made of Cruise Clubs. These are held each week to prepare children for the experience of a lifetime on board a floating school ship. The idea is to prepare the voyagers in such a way that they are able to gain the maximum amount from their short voyage, both in terms of the days at sea and the visits ashore when they dock. Some schools have now begun to apply the same principle to a trip to Europe. They have a regular meeting, possibly after school, when all aspects of the journey are thoroughly investigated and problems such as different currency, the appropriate clothing or how to take photographs are discussed and solved.

Party leaders usually supply their children with certain tasks to be done during the visit and these may best be recorded on worksheets. With the advent of photocopying machines, scanners and thermal stencils it is not too difficult to make these sheets attractive and even present them in the form of a little custom-made booklet. One such booklet designed for a trip to Belgium contained details of rates of exchange (1,000 Francs to £10); a map of the Low Countries; pages on visits planned; questions based on what was to be seen and a section on puzzles. It proved to be very interesting. The teacher should set aside a short time each day for this work and not make it too onerous a task. Don't kill that precious enthusiasm!

## Switzerland

A programme on television portrayed the life of a modern-day businessman and entrepreneur who lived in Switzerland and commuted from there to many parts of Europe. As a keen supporter of Stoke City Football Club he even drove to Britain whenever he could manage the time, to watch his favourite team and combine business with pleasure. For him, Switzerland was something like the ideal country and his view is shared by the writer Donald Cowie (1971) when he describes the land and the people of Switzerland. It's a far cry from the image we have from the stories of William Tell and the evil Geslar!

Imagine a competiton to decide what was the best country in the world. The judges would have to give points for certain attributes, such as standards of living, financial reserves, achievements in the arts, science and industry, also relative success in avoiding maladies of the body and mind ranging from malnutrition to sex troubles, wars and strikes. Beauty, cleanliness and efficiency of cities, towns and villages would be taken into account. Taxation, particularly of income and inheritances. Amount per head of population contributed to world charities. Quality of clothes, bathroom fittings, building materials. Longevity and infant mortality. Hospitality. Courtesy.

In such a test Switzerland would probably come at the top. She has those mountains that make her one of the most beautiful countries, and that also force her to work and play hard. The scenery is so bright on the eyes that it provides raw material for a lucrative tourist industry.

It is not surprising, therefore, to find that Switzerland has enjoyed an increasing popularity as a centre for accommodating parties of school children and their industrious teachers. But what a journey! The itinerary of a primary school's visit ran as follows:

| 23 May | Depart from Birmingham 1048 | Meal at café 1300 |
|--------|------------------------------|--------------------|
|        | Depart from Victoria 1535:   | Arrive at Dover 1725 |
|        | Depart from Dover 1800:      | Arrive at Calais 1930 |
| 24 May | Depart Calais 2012:          | Arrive at Basel 0520 |
|        | Arrive at Brig 0950:         | Depart from Brig 1000 |
|        | Arrive at Fiesch 1035        |                    |

And that was just to get there!

But there is a great deal to be learnt from the way the trip was actually organized and the arrangements made by the party leader Peter Greenwood, Headmaster of Turfpits Primary School, Erdington. Luckily, like all good trippers, he kept certain documents and it is to these that reference is now made in order to draw out some important points for those contemplating such an excursion.

1   The trip was arranged by Ultima Travel, specialists in school
    visits. They have one advantage over other firms in that they
    have experienced teachers on their staff and they work out
    trips with the children very much in mind. (Address: 424
    Chester Road, Little Sutton, Wirral, Cheshire)
2   The actual travel documents were kept in two separate
    folders – these were provided by the travel agents. In one were
    all the papers relating to the outward journey – meal
    bookings, rail tickets, telex information on trip bookings, etc.
    The other folder was reserved for the return journey and the
    copy of the timetable for trains and connections was
    transferred from the first folder to the second for the
    homeward travel.
3   The typewritten timetable was used as a checklist, points and
    duties *en route* being ticked off as they were disposed of.
4   The deputy leader Mr Jones was briefed from the very
    beginning of the trip arrangements. This meant that he knew
    roughly what was required and what would happen. (In the
    event this proved to be a godsend, for the leader was taken ill
    just before the return journey and the deputy leader had to
    take control of the party.)
5   The tickets were put in the order they were to be used – just
    one little way of making things easier.
6   To keep hands free for other things, all the relevant
    documents were carried slung in an old school satchel – *not*
    kept in a suitcase where they might be inaccessible just at the
    moment they were required.
7   Each group leader (and there were four for twenty-eight
    children) had a list of his group with names, addresses, etc.
    The leader did not have the responsibility of a group while
    travelling as he needed to be free to look around, find
    information and make decisions.

   The trip turned out to be an unqualified success and, in spite of
being taken ill, the leader would be quite happy to go again – and
so would the children. When they got to the holiday village in the
beautiful mountains, the children spent one day at ease on the
site, recovering from a long journey. They then enjoyed trips to
Zermatt, Brig, Andermatt and Kandersteg, meeting children
from practically every other country of Europe in this
breathtaking holiday centre, described in the brochures as 'the
modern centre for excursions, rambling and winter sports, an

ideal place for study, sports and skiing weeks, youth holiday camps, organized children's holidays, school Alpine holidays, weekend events, schools' and works' outings, conferences, etc.' The Swiss air and scenery cannot be bettered as an experience in itself, and the children had a marvellous time exploring a brand new environment.

Looking back over what happened, the teachers in charge thought of certain things which might be useful to the reader who has yet to go into Europe. These are now tabulated in note form.

1   There should be meetings with parents beforehand and group leaders should talk with their particular parents who can tell them private yet important things about their children.

2   It should be made clear that when one of the teachers tells a child to do something they should do it straightaway and without question. It may be a matter of life or death.

3   The staff are on the trip for the benefit of the children. They are on call twenty-four hours a day. Lazy or sciving teachers are useless.

4   Letters from home should be banned. Very often the children who receive them are more upset than those who don't. Telephone numbers may be given but they are strictly for emergencies only.

5   Some attempt should be made to copy the Swiss habit of cleanliness. Rooms should be kept tidy and hygiene emphasized.

6   Expect girls, however small in stature, to be more mature than boys – even if the boys are always acting big at school.

7   A European trip will give the teachers a chance to really get to know their children as people. They will confide in 'Sir' or 'Miss', and the unexpected will happen as children surprise their teachers by what they say, think and do.

8   Try to be 'young at heart'. If you don't try hard enough the trip will almost certainly be a failure. Children are energetic: they expect the teachers to be the same. Work hard certainly, but play hard too.

9   The worst example a teacher can give is to be caught by the customs. Teachers must set standards for the children to emulate.

10   Take an interest in the children. Treat their shopping expeditions as important and help them to choose suitable

presents. These must be looked after, if necessary locked up, and carefully packed for the return journey.

11    Don't allow the party to be put on separate boats at the Channel ports. One school did that and lost a child to a different destination. When you are on the boat stay together and keep away from the side.

12    Arrange a telephone relay to advise the parents of your time of arrival on the way back. Watch out for children's table manners in public. Make fairly strict rules with regard to the eating of sweets.

**References**

BARRELL, G. R. (1975) *Teachers and the Law* Methuen

COWIE, D. (1971) *Switzerland: The Land and the People* Yoseloff

PASSPORT OFFICE (1972) *United Kingdom Collective Passport Application Form* available from Area Passport Offices

Chapter 8

# A life on the ocean wave

In 1936 a young teacher in Liverpool, Mr E. Heelas, accompanied his first school party on an educational cruise. Forty years later and, as this book was being written, Mr E. Heelas, now the retired Chief Inspector of the City of Birmingham Education Committee was once again aboard ship in the Mediterranean and convinced that cruising should remain one of the regular options of the school curriculum. As an educational experience, there is nothing wrong with life on board a specially adapted cruise ship and it is interesting to note that many seasoned travellers prefer to seek the company and the enthusiasm of children rather than to travel alone in a luxury liner. A ship is a place for meeting people, for exchanging views and sharing new experiences. Travel broadens the mind and a combination of new faces, fresh places and the company of intelligent people helps to make life on board a floating school quite different to any other experience.

The late Sir John Newsom was no stranger to the educational cruise ship and he wrote of his unforgettable experiences in the *Times Educational Supplement* (12 June, 1970). Later in that year he attempted to describe the educational significance of cruising and how it enriched the lives of those lucky enough to be involved. In the following paragraph from *Boarders Away* (Ollis 1973), he puts the concept of an educational cruise into perspective and helps to dispel the idea that a cruise is merely a holiday:

Almost inevitably the concept of a sea-going school is difficult to comprehend. This is especially so if 'education' is defined in the narrow terms of classroom experience geared to a particular syllabus designed to satisfy external examiners. This is a pompous way of describing 'school' solely or mainly concerned with the acquisition of factual knowledge and particular mental and physical skills. Of course this is an important part of the operation but the adequate development of the adolescent young involves a good deal more. A further difficulty is the average emotional response to the word 'cruise'. To most people this implies a 'holiday', the antithesis of 'work', a view supported by much of the glossy promotion material put out by shipping companies to attract custom for this, to be fair, most usual interpretation of the word. Is it possible to 'cruise' and 'work' simultaneously? I believe it is and that the British India Company have demonstrated it beyond doubt.

There is a great demand for places on school ships even though a tour may now cost over £100 and it is quite commonplace for children of primary school age to take part in a cruise which has been planned with their interests and needs very much in mind. If this were a history book it would be possible to go back over ten years to a time when just a handful of Birmingham primary schools participated in a cruise to Scandinavia or North Africa: it would be necessary to trace the development of cruising and its growing popularity with the schools: it would also be important to show how the idea of combining air travel to the point of embarkation in, say, Athens, had very quickly brought new perspectives and possibilities to cruising. But now that the 'Fly Cruise' is with us and cruising has an established popularity, it is probably far more fruitful to look at how a cruise is planned, what happens on board ship and at ports of call and, more particularly, what the teacher has to do if he finds himself lucky enough to be a party leader.

**Preparing for the big occasion**
Very, very early on Sunday morning, 21 May, a fleet of Corporation buses will set out from their garages collecting school parties from all districts of Birmingham and taking them to New Street Station.

There are two special trains to take the children to Southampton, the second train leaving about forty-five minutes after the first.

The first train will arrive at Southampton at

approximately 10.00 hours and will run alongside the *Nevasa* which will be waiting at the Dock.

It was with these words that the Cruise Book introduced the 1972 Birmingham Junior Schools Cruise to Madeira. The book itself was designed and collated by a group of Birmingham teachers with the express purpose of being a resource and information book for all the children and teachers who were going on the spring cruise to sunnier climes. Every child was given a copy and the book was used to prepare the children for the sort of experiences they would probably meet *en route*. Needless to say, it took many hours of meetings and research before the final draft of the text was agreed upon and then more effort and planning was put into producing the book by means of electronic scanner and electric duplicator. But the final production was custom-made for the particular cruise with relevant illustrations and appropriate facts and figures.

Planning the cruise at city level when there are fifty different schools involved is a mammoth task which resembles a military maneuvre. Every possible factor is taken into account to ensure success and efficiency. The organizers work after the manner of the painters on the Forth Bridge – as soon as one cruise is under way, they start to plan the next one. Nothing is left to chance. Every group has its party leader and every leader is programmed to do certain tasks on certain days. Once the overall planning has been done and strategies are agreed, each individual teacher will start the long process of preparation which ensures that the children will know where they are going, what will be required of them and what they have to look out for. It really is a massive undertaking. Landlubbers have to be introduced to the whole new world of the mariner. 'Port' suddenly becomes the left side and a staircase or ladder will be referred to as a 'companion way'. Even time will be signified by bells and an officer's job can be determined by the markings on his sleeves.

A great deal of work will be done in the school classroom long before the children ever see their ship – in this case the *Nevasa*, which was once a troop ship and was converted at the cost of a million pounds.

Some schools build up to the actual cruise by running a weekly club after school when points of interest are discussed. These could range from the rate of exchange or the common phrases of a foreign language to what sort of distinguishing clothing will be made for the particular school party. To reap the full benefit of the educational experience, both preparatory work and follow-up get-togethers are most valuable. In Birmingham it became almost traditional for the cruising fraternity to meet in the autumn to share their slides and reminiscences. The BBC film 'And Teddy Came Too' was a fine record of what can be achieved through the communal experience of a cruise.

### Pocket money

Pocket money can be a divisive element on any school venture. Some parents give their children too much money, thinking, in their naivety, that they are doing their children a favour, but it only makes it harder for the teacher who is trying to maintain order and morale. It is a good rule to insist that every child has the same amount of money. Pocket money can be included in the trip costs and then, with suitable banking arrangements, small sums can be given out at each port of call in the appropriate currency. Many children will waste money: others will hoard it. That's a part of the process of worldly maturity. Once again, careful preparation before the event can help children to conserve their pocket money. Films and airletters can be bought at home and used on board. That may be one way of ensuring that parents hear from their children and have at least one picture to record the happenings!

### A cruise lover's checklist

It is difficult to do justice to the complex experience of an educational cruise; certainly not in a few sentences! Richard Broughton (Deputy Head at Lyndhurst Primary School) is an experienced teacher-cruiser, and he offers some notes for those who are contemplating a cruise or who may find themselves elected as a party leader for the first time.

'It is said that the unscrupulous spivs and wideboys who pose as Moroccan traders deliberately sell infested pouffes and cushions to cruise children knowing full well that, once back on board ship, and away from the dockside, these articles will be thrown overboard by teachers and crew – only to be washed ashore on the next tide, dried out and then resold to more gullible souvenir hunters. An apocryphal story, but one which serves to emphasize a point. Newcomers can easily be caught out. For the key to successful cruising – as in all other aspects of teaching – is preparation. But, because cruising entails more expense, more learning situations and much more risk, it involves even more detailed preparation. There is little or no margin of error and one simple miscalculation or oversight can ruin what should be a child's greatest experience.

'The cruise preparation begins about one year before the ship actually weighs anchor. The only ship currently operating educational cruises from the UK is British India's *SS Uganda* and for the purpose of these notes the terms "ship" and *Uganda* will be synonymous. As soon as it has been agreed that the school will send a party of a suitable size, say fifteen to thirty children, a meeting is arranged in school where the prospective party leader has the opportunity to explain the educational cruise idea in detail to the parents as well as the children. If the party leader has cruised before he will have a personal collection of items with which to illustrate his talk. If not, and if this is the first time, films, charts, photographs and other material is available from British India, the shipping company. The serious business of preparation can then begin and for convenience of description this can be divided into two parts – the technical and the educational aspects of preparation.

TECHNICAL PREPARATION
'Technical preparation may be defined as that essential preparation which will ensure that, on the day of embarkation, all the necessary legal steps have been taken to allow the party to pursue its journey. It is best considered under various headings.

(a) *Collection of money*
'Most parents prefer to pay by weekly instalments on a set day each week. So each child will need a paying-in card which acts as a receipt and a record of payment. All the money received in school must be paid into a bank account – preferably a deposit account where it will gain a small amount of interest. An initial deposit of £10 is payable to British India for each child booked on to a cruise. They will inform you of the date for final payment of the balance of fares.

(b) *Vaccination and inoculation*
'Some cruises, especially those travelling to Africa and Asia Minor necessitate the vaccination of all members of the cruise parties. British India will advise when and if this is applicable. Vaccination certificates must be obtained for all the children and

kept safely and, in the case of those children who for reasons of religion or health cannot be vaccinated, a letter from a doctor or parent to this effect is also necessary.

(c)  *Passports and identity cards*
'Party leaders must have a full United Kingdom passport. Some older children and children of foreign nationals may well have their own passports, but most children will travel on a group passport obtainable through the Passport Office. Three identical copies are necessary. Some countries demand an identity card for each child in conjunction with the group passport. Each card has to carry a passport-size photograph of the child. Sometimes the school photographer will do these for you as a part of his public relations and business efficiency programme! There are more words about this aspect in the chapter on Europe.

(d)  *Diets and medical problems*
'There is no reason why children with dietary problems need be excluded from a cruise party. This applies equally to children who have other non-serious medical problems. *SS Uganda* can cope with special diets and is equipped with a hospital and operating theatre. However, it is imperative that all such problems are known to party leaders and British India well before sailing dates. No medicaments, whether on prescription or not, may be taken aboard by any pupil. They must be given to the party leader who will, in turn, hand them over to the ship's medical staff.

'A quite common occurrence, which could pose problems, is that of mature girls experiencing periods during the cruise. It could be awkward and embarrassing if the party leader is a male so he must ensure that his relationship with the girls in his party and their parents is of the type in which neither he nor the girls will be concerned too much if it should be that time. The mothers should know whether or not this is likely to happen during the cruise and the girl should take a supply of towels with her. They can be bought on ship but this is an expensive drain on precious pocket money.

(e)  *Medical examination*
'No child is allowed to travel on an educational cruise ship without a prior medical examination and clearance from the school medical officer. This should be arranged by the party leader in conjunction with the local school clinic and a Certificate

of Medical Seaworthiness must be obtained for every member of the party.

## (f)  *Form filling and documentation*
'Throughout the long period of preparation for the cruise, party leaders will find that certain procedures must be completed and certain forms will be required by certain dates. To avoid confusion of the "when do I have to do what" variety, it is useful to keep a separate one-sheet calendar on which to record the necessary dates by which certain actions must be taken. By the time the cruise date arrives the teacher will find himself in the possession of a great number of documents – of greater and lesser importance. The writer has always kept these in separate folders – one for all the essential documents (passports, vaccination certificates, medical certificates, addresses and phone numbers) and another for the remainder.

EDUCATIONAL PREPARATION
'Educational preparation is also a vast subject which is best looked at from different angles.

## (a)  *Ship's routine*
'SS Uganda is a floating boarding school and children must be well briefed on the system which operates on board. The smooth running of the ship really depends upon each child's continuous awareness of its responsibilities. For example, a party arriving twenty minutes late for lunch might cause an enormous confusion if they are called to disembark for a shore excursion whilst still in the middle of rhubarb pie and custard. Each child must be made fully aware of what cruising involves *before* sailing: that it is *not* a holiday but, instead, a rather exciting way of furthering his educational experience.

'Before the great adventure begins, a responsible party leader will have ensured that each child has certain facts indelibly imprinted on his mind. These should include his dormitory name and colour (dormitory sections are colour-coded for easy location), his classroom name, his group number and his school code letters. Each child must remember to listen patiently to every single announcement that comes over the public address system. It is amazing how many rumbling tummies are the result of missing a meal due to inattention to announcements broadcast that way. That is not too serious, but missing a call to disembarkation will be the source of confusion as teacher dashes madly around trying to find the unfortunate offender.

## (b)   *Preparation for excursions*
'Stepping ashore for the first time in a new country is what cruising is all about. It is even more rewarding for the group that has been well prepared for the moment of truth.

'The duration of each shore visit varies between six hours and thirty-six hours – depending upon the size and importance of the port of call. During the longer stops students return to *Uganda* for meals and sleeping. It is the duty of the party leader to ensure that his children extract the most benefit from these excursions. They must know what to look for and the significance of what they find. The teacher will be asked a hundred or more questions and some will be very awkward ones about things which are seen by the children (pornography shops in Copenhagen; contraceptive machines in Sweden or the excretory habits of some of the natives of Northern Africa). The party leader can help himself by arranging a bulk loan of suitable travel books from the local library and these will assist the preparation. If other schools in your area are going, get in quickly or, like Mother Hubbard, you might find the appropriate shelves empty. Embassies or tourist offices of most countries are usually willing to supply colourful brochures and posters and some will even hire out films. Schools which have been on a cruise very often make their own cine records and these are a valuable source for future cruises. Making a film could be one way of sharing the flavour of the cruise with those who were left at home. British India supply charts which show cut-away diagrams of the ship, illustrations of parts of the *Uganda* and information on nautical terms and emblems. The book *Boarders Away* is a valuable resource which should be purchased by the enterprising teacher.

## (c)   *Communal scrap-books*
'These home-made cruise record books are a meaningful way of ensuring that all the children become involved in the preparation and share in the account of what happened which will later be so very interesting to the parents and all those at school who didn't go abroad. A good idea is to sectionalize these books as under:

1   Looking forward to the cruise
The children are asked to write freely of their anticipation of the

cruise. Poems are sought or made up about the sea, ships and foreign parts. The section will also include some details of the preparation – the unpleasant as well as the pleasant parts.

## 2   The *SS Uganda*

This section includes mostly illustrations concerning the ship. Each picture is pasted into the scrap-book and a suitable space is left beside it for a written description to be added during the cruise when it can be a result of first-hand experience. Such descriptive passages can be used in conjunction with pictures of the dormitories, cafeteria, canteen, classrooms, lecture theatre, games areas, the bridge and so on.

## 3   The ports of call

Each cruise will involve several shore excursions and each port of call merits a separate subsection in the scrap-book. Work can be divided into two parts: one part will deal with the country being visited and the other with the specific port. Information about the destination country is available and preparatory work should include details of population, the religious practices, climate, national dress and customs and currency. A few simple phrases from the native tongue are easy to learn, even in Greek or Turkish. It's surprising how pleased souvenir shop owners can be when children say "Thank you" in their own language. Details on the port may be a good deal harder to find but any available information can be pasted into the book, leaving plenty of space for written and art work produced in classroom periods after the shore visit. Bus tickets, shop receipts and decorative wrappings, matchbox covers, postcards, newspapers and other such memorabilia help to improve the quality and usefulness of the final scrap-book.

## 4   Ships and the sea

The educational experience of cruising concerns all aspects of the venture and this will include work about the various types of ship encountered, how to recognize each variety and what they do. It will also include work on lightships, buoys, lighthouses and the lifeboat service; maybe even a section on maritime travel which will help to explain the style and design of certain native ships seen in foreign inshore waters.

## (d)   *What to take with you for work on board ship*

'There is no limit to the amount of luggage a party leader can take

H

on the cruise. Therefore, no teacher need omit personal luggage in order to take suitable material for classroom work. So an extra suitcase might be used for the following items:

Lined exercise paper in two different sizes
Plain exercise paper for drawing
Paste in a polythene bottle with the top secured and fixed with Sellotape
A roll of Sellotape
Two pencils per child and two sharpeners
Half a dozen rubbers
One large and six small pairs of scissors
A good set of felt-tip pens
Packets of paperclips and split pins.

One should not forget a simple first aid kit to go with these essentials. It should contain Elastoplast, cotton wool, lint, Dettol, TCP, Savlon, some bandages, polythene bags in case of coach sickness and paper tissues.'

ON BOARD SHIP
So there you are on board ship with a group of lively energetic children. What is the day's programme going to be? How many constraints are there to prevent you doing what you want or to make you conform? The shipboard programme is analysed by our cruise adviser Richard Broughton.

'The day spent aboard ship, as opposed to the one which includes a shore visit, will be split into six periods of about forty-five minutes' duration: four before the midday meal and two afterwards. These periods are then spent in one of four separate activities, according to the exigencies of the timetable:

1  Classroom periods
2  Lecture hall periods
3  Private study sessions
4  Games and recreation lessons

'Each of these may be described in more detail in an attempt to put the uninitiated into the picture.

1  *Classroom periods*
It is during these periods, one or two during a complete day aboard, that the well-prepared party leader will produce written

114

and illustrative work from his group. They should be asked to write about personal experiences, things which they enjoyed seeing and doing rather than those things which, perhaps, they were expected to see and found less exciting. Directions to children should be specific rather than the "write about what you did yesterday" type. The best pieces of work will be included in the communal scrap-book. During the cruise every member of the group must contribute to this effort, even though the standard of some of these pieces of work may not be of the highest order.

## 2   Lecture hall periods

During these sessions the staff of *Uganda* give talks to the children about the ship and the ports of call. These are illustrated by film slides and films of the places, and the staff are most expert at keeping the children interested and in whetting their appetites for the adventure to come. Children are allotted specific seats in the lecture theatre to avoid unnecessary scrambling to forward seats and the theatre doubles as a cinema in the evenings.

## 3   Private study sessions

These periods are for children to do their own private work such as writing letters home or filling in their diaries. The ship provides children with a diary/logbook for which a prize is presented towards the end of the cruise.

## 4   Games and recreation lessons

Certain parts of the decks of *Uganda* are marked out for games such as deck hockey, quoits, handball and shuffleboard. Materials are stored in the PE locker and drawn by party leaders at the start of each session – and then returned afterwards. The rules of each game are explained in the "Notes for Party Leaders" supplied by the shipping company, but these do not have to be strictly adhered to. The best games are often invented by the children. Incidentally, hockey and handball are played with rope quoits, not with balls.

'For organizational reasons the nine hundred children are divided into six groups – each child being supplied with a badge showing their group number as well as another showing their dormitory name and muster station for lifeboat drill. Each evening the timetable for the following day is given to party leaders. A typical timetable would appear like this:

| | Time | Assembly hall | Classrooms | Private study | Deck games |
|---|---|---|---|---|---|
| 1 | 0900–0945 | III and IV | V and VI | II | I |
| 2 | 1000–1045 | V and VI | I and II | IV | III |
| 3 | 1100–1145 | I and II | III and IV | V | VI |
| 4 | 1200–1245 | III and IV | V and VI | I | II |
| 5 | 1400–1445 | V and VI | I and II | III | IV |
| 6 | 1500–1545 | I and II | III and IV | VI | V |

'It is essential that, at all times, the children in the party should be kept active. For most children on the cruise it will be their first time away from parents, brothers and sisters and even pets. Continual activities keep their minds off such things and helps them to avoid homesickness. The shipboard life provides plenty of leisure activities in "off duty" hours (fairs, sports days, discos, games, competitions and singsongs) and the children should be encouraged to indulge in them all. There is no better incentive to participate than to see the teacher letting his or her hair down to a "pop record" – especially if that teacher is suitably dressed in a monkey suit or long evening dress. Children should be persuaded to take one set of "sharp" clothes for social events such as these.'

## Privilege

Many teachers are against the cruise because they feel it smacks of privilege. Only a few children can go and selection depends upon the ability of the parents to pay the necessary expenses. The strange thing is that many children from comparatively poor homes do actually go on cruises. The parents have the best part of a year to save the money by weekly instalments and somehow they manage it. Looking through the names of the schools that travelled on the Madeira Cruise in 1972 one is struck by the fact that many of the city's inner-ring schools did take part. As Mr Heelas himself said, 'With a year to pay, many secondary school pupils take a part-time job – perhaps a few hours a week – and earn the money to cover their costs. What better way could there be to encourage initiative, responsibility and a sense of purpose.' Life is like that. Not everyone can have everything which he wants and it may be that sacrifices will have to be made if a cruise trip is to be made possible. The statistics show that it is not the 'idle rich' – if there are any of them left – who monopolize educational cruises. Many very ordinary families scattered over all parts of

Britain find ways and means of sending their children to Athens, Casablanca, Venice or Copenhagen.

The question 'What do the children get out of the cruise?' may be a very difficult one to answer, for so much depends upon the individual child. If the child is going merely so that his family can keep up with the Joneses – because it's 'the done thing' – then he might not gain a great deal. But if the cruise event is the result of careful preparation and eager expectation, then the communal travel on a floating school will undoubtedly yield a rich harvest.

It looks very much as if cruises are here to stay and, in spite of the criticisms to the contrary, are beginning to have a more universal appeal. In *Boarders Away* (Ollis 1973) one reads the following comment:

> Clearly a change has come over our system. What was so recently an affair for the children of better-off parents is slowly going into the curriculum for every boy and girl at school. And money is being found for it. This of course is what must happen, once the LEA is directly involved. It may not be long before we have a democratic system of school travel and international experience, right across the country.

**Reflections**
Many teachers who have actually taken children on board ship and lived a close life with them during the voyage have nothing but praise for the idea of a cruise as a shared educational experience. The points of view and reminiscences which follow are very convincing.

Elwyn Jackson is Headmaster of Yenton Junior School, Birmingham, and has been involved with cruising for at least ten years. He writes the following reminiscences.

'Cruising aboard a fully equipped luxury liner with programmed visits and exotic ports of call has long been regarded as the lifestyle and prerogative of the rich, the ambition of the newly retired executive or, perhaps, the reward of the fortunate "pools" winner. One equates cruising with play and relaxation, comfort and style, adventure and entertainment and, above all, as the complete antithesis of mental and physical exertion. Indeed, the emotive quality of the prose to be found in any cruise brochure invites a person to participate in each and every one of the amenities which are offered aboard the floating hotel and everything is geared to persuade the would-be voyager to relax and enjoy himself and to forget all about the common heritage – work.

'So how can one justify taking a thousand children on board ship? The immediate thought that springs to mind is that the children are learning – they are gaining first-hand experience and knowledge of an extended environment. This cannot be denied. Every day, throughout the land, children are taken on educational trips and journeys to places of interest. It is an integral part of the school curriculum. The innovation of environmental studies as a subject or an approach, the growing awareness of the need for conservation and the worldwide concern over pollution have awakened in us as teachers and parents the need to extend the children's interests and activities far beyond the classroom confines. By taking them out of school, teachers are helping to make children aware of their responsibility to their environment whilst they also derive valuable experience and benefits from such visits.

'The ship has been converted into a floating school. This is the operative phrase and the one to remember – the ramifications of work, knowledge, experience and interest, albeit in pleasant and new surroundings, distinguish the educational discovery cruise from the holiday cruise. They also give credence to the view that it is a working holiday for both teachers and children. Many will long remember, nostalgically, visits to Lisbon, Tangiers, Casablanca, Istanbul, Venice and Naples. They will have seen Etna, Vesuvius or Stromboli, climbed the Acropolis to view the famous Parthenon and will be able to speak with authority on Saint Mark's Square and the Doges Palace. To experience things at first hand is far more valuable than knowledge to be gained from books, and teachers testify to the increased vitality of their teaching when they have actually been to places for themselves.

'The cruise arrangements are like a military maneuvre –nothing is to be left to chance. Likewise the preparation is intensive, for this is to be a complete educational experience. In Birmingham a cruise book is written specially for each cruise. It gives facts about the ship, life on board and background information on the ports of call. It also serves a threefold purpose: it is a workbook, a source of information and then is coveted by the children as a souvenir of the actual cruise. Uniformity of dress for the shore visits has a practical as well as an aesthetic purpose. When the children are ashore they can be more easily identified when walking together through busy market streets and their colourful headgear distinguishes them from the local populace. The sight of a thousand children on the side of the quay, resplendent in their multicoloured uniforms, and the impeccable behaviour abroad brought many favourable comments from private passengers and a hint of pride to the eyes of their party leaders.

'Jerome K. Jerome's amusing account of three men in Hampton Court maze could well be taken as an illustration of the party leaders' attempts to find a way through the veritable labyrinth of passages aboard ship. Down below, one could never be sure in which direction the ship was travelling and whether one was on A, B or C deck. But almost from the moment the children were aboard they could be relied upon to give explicit directions to the assembly hall and the library, the recreation room and the tuck shop from any point on the ship. An early start from school and a long first day's journey to the port failed to subdue the mounting excitement of bedtime on the first night. A great deal of animated chatter filled the dormitories and it was a long time before visits to the toilet diminished into mere trickles and a restless peace descended upon the ship. Then, teddies and other favourite bedtime companions, smuggled aboard, would appear from beneath pillows and bedclothes to be clutched diffidently by the boys until overriding fatigue brought its own kind of tranquility.

'At 9.30 pm, when the Master at Arms took over the supervision of the dormitories, the teachers were free to enjoy the amenities afforded to all the other passengers. Most retired early to prepare for the very full day ahead, which would begin in the dormitories at 7.30 am, where children required help of one form or another. Left to their own resources and without the threat of an inspection by the captain one shudders to think what state the ship would be in within a few days. But this is also a part of the exercise and the children showed a great pride when their marks out of ten steadily increased.

'The timetable on board was a formidable one, yet necessary if a thousand children were to be controlled and taught with a minimum of fuss. It continued almost relentlessly whilst at sea, broken occasionally by the Tannoy when the captain announced the sighting of a school of whales or the passing of a British cruiser on the port bow. At such moments everyone would congregate at the nearest vantage point to see what was happening and to learn from the new experience.

'But the cruise highlights were the shore visits – a chance to be free of lessons (which child wouldn't agree with this) and the opportunity to leave the confines of the ship and spend some foreign money. In many countries it gave the children the chance to try out the delicate art of bartering. How proud they were to display the goods they had acquired at "knockdown" prices. A walk down the Casbah is a never-to-be-forgotten experience. Many children had visited Europe, but this was something entirely different. This was the East. They walked down the narrow, silent streets with some trepidation. Veiled women withdrew and remonstrated angrily at the appearance of a camera. Colourful water-sellers signified their presence with the sounding of a bell. Child beggars leading crippled and sightless relatives with dejected, pale faces, thrust their begging bowls before the children. Strange smells, mysterious foods and unfamiliar voices enveloped the senses as the children looked at a new world.

'Back on board and away to new places: Lisbon, city of statues, the Salazar Bridge and the River Tagus. Yet another shopping expedition and a tour of the city – a thousand children don a thousand costumes and the sea is suddenly alive with laughing children and fifty party leaders wondering how to shepherd them safely to the waiting coaches. On a southern cruise the children will have travelled 2,000 miles or more by sea and learned of a new way of life by people of many lands. It is an introduction to life's rich pattern at an early age.

'On return to school there will be a parents' evening to show films and a selection of the many slides and pictures taken. Two of the children will give a commentary and amaze everyone with their detailed knowledge and anecdotes. The success or failure of the venture will be judged, not in terms of knowledge or facts learnt, but rather as an experience in living together – an adventure in life.'

A WOMAN'S POINT OF VIEW

But what does the teacher think about cruising? It is difficult to generalize, but Beryl Dare, Headmistress of Hawthorn School, Birmingham, offers her point of view based upon a considerable experience of educational trips aboard the British India vessels.

'Being a party leader aboard ship for the first time seems almost to submerge one in a welter of confusion, with no sense of direction, and in the dormitory, beset with the allocation of lockers and the unpacking of clothes, one is interrupted with a multitude of "Please Miss" questions for which there seem to be no answers. Just to complicate this, there is the voice of the Tannoy for which one quickly develops a love-hate relationship as it instructs school A to go to point B: by this time school A has scattered to all parts of the ship and the teacher has very little idea where point B is.

'But for me, the next stage is very important. I find the haven of my own cabin and, whilst waiting for my luggage to arrive, I ponder the events of the last twenty-four hours. Did I leave enough food for my son? Did I remind him to wash the cat's dishes regularly? Would he remember to lock up the house before retiring for the night? By now, I am rather tense and quite certain that my luggage is lost. I think back to the many pre-cruise shopping expeditions, of selection and rejection, something new and smart – evening wear for gracious dining and lively dances – slacks and sweaters for deck wear.

'If my case is lost, the cruise will be spoiled for me. Then there is a knock on the door and a white coated Indian cabin steward comes in and smilingly says "Mem sa here is your case". At last, all is well!

'Now to unpack, to be concerned over creases, to wonder whether one has brought too much or, again, perhaps too little. The very act of unpacking, putting away and hanging up clothes, by the very nature of its orderliness seems, for a woman, to dispel the confusion of the early arrival, and in the nature of things one finds oneself wandering off to the lounge for a cup of tea and to exchange early impressions with colleagues who have also been beset by the same sense of confusion.

'Heavens – I've forgotten to make a hair appointment for Ladies Night. I must do this before the party leaders' conference which commences shortly.

'Somehow, as if by magic, the party leaders' conference turns the jigsaw of confusion into a quite orderly pattern. The welcome by the captain, the talk given by the ship's headmaster and matron and the daily programme of organization seem to transmute a foreign environment into a "School at Sea". We are once more on familiar ground.

'And so for all party leaders the routine develops of not just "a school at sea" but "a boarding school at sea" and it is the "boarding" part that emphasizes, in many ways, the function of the woman party leader.

'Just as, with the family, the mother becomes identified with the "looking after", the "comforting and the care" of children, so does the woman party leader become the temporary mother of the party. It is, indeed, a very wonderful opportunity for the woman party leader to get close to the children in a way that she never could at school. In return, the children lean on her and, perhaps, take her for granted, just as they do their own mother. They also see the woman teacher in a slightly different light. They are interested in her wardrobe. They love to see her in evening wear at the children's nightly disco and, again, at bedtime. They also love to join with her in shopping; the girls, in particular, enjoy appraising with her shopping costs and clothing styles in different parts of the world.

'When the Fancy Dress Parade is imminent, one is expected to produce the necessary make-up to transform the "little dears" into "Miss *Uganda*" or a bearded captain. After six cruises with children I still forget to take some cheap cosmetics with me for the purpose and I end up with no lipstick and broken eyebrow pencils.

'But for me, as a woman, an educational cruise is a combination of several things. During the long working day it is intensified teaching and mothering, and at night there is the opportunity for a style of gracious living that becomes rarer in the hustle and bustle of our busy modern pace of life.'

### A final word

It would appear from all that has been written that 'the cruise is the thing'. The same ingredients for success apply in cruising as in other out-of-school activities. Good preparation and hard work lead to a successful conclusion. But the two key words for party leaders are really 'imagination' and 'resourcefulness'. It is no good going on a cruise if you want a quiet and uneventful ten days, and most teachers return from the voyage ready for a good sleep, and to relax and unwind out of the sight of children. The effort has been tremendous, but somehow it has all seemed worthwhile.

The main thing about the cruise is that it has helped to broaden the experience of the travellers – to widen their horizons. Travel does have an effect on people – leading them to a wider vision of life, and there is no substitute for this kind of awakening. Geography, history, politics and economics suddenly assume some sort of meaning when they are translated into the reality of the Tivoli Gardens or a Moroccan market-place. There may be some fresh incentive to learn a foreign language when one has struggled to express a desire or to understand a meaning. Life on board ship, at the mercy of the mighty ocean, does a great deal to impress the idea that man is but small and of little consequence compared to the God-inspired forces of nature.

Most of the teachers who have been on cruises are convinced of their great educational value. Setbacks such as seasickness or dormitory patrol have soon been forgotten when compared to the tremendous feeling of fellowship and camaraderie that has been created during the voyage and on shore visits at the ports of call.

Perhaps the final word should come from an experienced teacher-cruiser, Ronald Gould. Writing in *Boarders Away* (Ollis 1973), he had this to say about the imaginative experiences of a cruise:

> The strict order and discipline of a ship, combined with the discipline of a boarding-school life is another useful experience, for it becomes obvious to all that order and discipline in such conditions, and perhaps in others, are essential for safety and well-being. And who could doubt that life is richer after contact with the lives and cultures of others? At any rate, I cherish the happiest memories of a school cruise and life for me is richer for that experience.

**Reference**
OLLIS, M. (1973) *Boarders Away* Longman

Chapter 9

# Just for the record

As has already been stressed, school journeys fit into many different categories according to their scope and purpose. The range extends from taking children in small groups into the locality of the school just to see something mundane, to taking a large group of children from many different schools half way round the world. But whatever the journey, there is one unifying factor: children learn from their new experience. Even a trip planned purely as a holiday does a great deal towards widening horizons and broadening the child's education. Children will learn from a journey almost in spite of the teacher, but if the teacher makes it his business to follow up the experience there will be plenty of opportunity for meaningful classroom work. The interest of a journey brings with it that motivation which is so important in the pursuit of enthusiasm. But the wise teacher will take care to vary the follow-up diet. Otherwise children will go out of school thinking to themselves, 'Oh dear, we shall have to write about it when we get back!', and the precious quality of adventure and freshness will be forever lost.

But how should a journey be recorded? Is it of any use keeping a record? Why should we bother? Can't we leave the journey to make its own impact? Which is the most useful way of preserving the experience for posterity? These and a dozen more questions cross the mind when one considers the sequel to a school trip.

Recently some children returned to school from a trip to the cathedral city of Worcester which had included a river trip. For some of them the highlight had been to travel on a boat with a bar and drink ginger-beer; for others it had been talking to a monkish figure in the confines of the cathedral and looking at the desolation and decay of the crypt. Each boy and girl had a fund of memories to look back on and it proved to be a very happy trip.

124

Next day the children redoubled their efforts to produce their own accounts of the day. Using a large sheet of manilla card each child set to work to make drawings, to add written reminiscences and, perhaps, to enrich their wall reports with a little research on some item that had taken their fancy. The variety of the approach and the fact that the work was written up to display for parents and others to see gave the end-product a certain richness and quality in addition to its originality.

On another day trip – this time to the Ironbridge Gorge – a ten year old boy took the school's cassette recorder. At certain points along the way he paused either to interview people or to record a comment. At the museum he described some of the items of industrial archaeology and even crawled into one of the old furnaces where he envisaged working conditions at the time of the Industrial Revolution. It might not have been all that accurate, but it served as the basis for a radio programme in which the experience was shared with the rest of the school. The one big advantage of using the cassette recorder is that it is instantly available. Being battery operated it can be taken easily on a trip and used almost anywhere as a simple but effective means of keeping a record of sounds and voices. These can then be stored and used later as a resource for further work and investigation. It also has one drawback: if the teacher fails to keep cool or is a little indiscreet with his comments they may be recorded on tape for posterity – to be used later as evidence against him – so check your tapes before they are used for a public hearing.

Making a cine film is an art form in itself. If you decide to keep a record of a moment of importance, then make sure the person who operates the camera is not a complete novice. The author once made a tolerably good film of a school trip to Belgium. It was used as a means of showing the parents what happened on the trip and also as a way of advertising the next trip to Belgium. In contrast the film taken of a wet week in the Welsh mountains was a very poor effort and when someone borrowed the camera to film a cruise the results were completely negative. (Did they remember to take the lens hood off the camera?) Once again, be prepared. Is the school projector standard eight or super eight? It's not much good spending money on the film if you can't show it afterwards. But don't be put off by thoughts of inadequacy. Once you have used a cine camera it can become a hobby – if not a habit – and you will have to guard against filming things for the sake of it. It's good fun and it brings a sense of achievement. The school resource centre or cupboard would benefit from the multi-media approach.

Polaroid cameras are a very useful resource. The children like to use them and they are one way of making an instant record of events. The picture can be used for a scrap-book or diary and it has the advantage of being instantly available for discussion and comment, and for making comparisons at a later date. If you buy a Polaroid camera get the latest machine so that the film needs no application of fixing chemicals. But remember the limitations. If you want more than one copy of a snap then take it with a camera which will provide you with a negative. It's much cheaper in the long run. Keep your Polaroid camera as an 'instant resource'; it will bring realism to your project record by capturing certain moments exactly as the eye would have seen them.

Most infant classes go, at some time or other, to the zoo. It gives them the chance to see the animals which really have only a storybook reality for most children living in suburbia. One of the best ways to record such a visit is on slides. The Kodak Instamatic camera is a delight. It is very simple to use. All you do is look in the viewfinder, decide on your picture and press the button. The completed film is sent off to the Kodak laboratories and usually returns within the week. For those who like to keep a record of places and faces these slide cameras are absolutely ideal. At a later date the staff can load up the projector, view the slides, and decide whether they want to go to that place again. Pictures bring back memories far better than anything else. By carefully selecting a programme of slides it is possible to relive a journey, to advertise it to others and to illustrate lesson topics from actual events and places associated with the school and the children. In some ways slides are the best of all recording devices and every school should possess at least one simple 35mm camera. The Pocketmatic range is ideal for anyone who wants to store pictures in the smallest possible spaces and there may be a good argument in these days of conservation for putting records on film instead of on paper.

But whilst multi-media resources have been adopted as a part of the new educational technology approach, there is still room for the more conventional record. Each trip organizer should keep a copy of the documents relating to a trip, journey or project in a special folder. Ideally this would be filed away for future reference. The children might also make a folder, a diary, a notebook or a scrap-book record of events. But try to vary the approach. For example, on their first study trip to Oxford some children made books with specific topics: Blenheim Palace; a survey of the Headington Area, or 'Our journey from home'. On a second journey they were persuaded to keep a notebook or diary. Both books were specially made to suit their purpose with different kinds of paper sewn in to cover every known requirement. Children take pride in a book if it is their own private special treasure. Although the teacher should see the work and check that it is to the required standard it is, perhaps, rather unkind and certainly very off-putting if he covers it with corrections and comments. There is a case for leaving the books unmarked – though not unseen – if the precious quality of enthusiasm is to be safeguarded. Most primary children like to illustrate their pages with sketches, drawings and illustrations. Felt-tips and pencil crayons are useful additions to the classroom equipment. Painting pictures in books is not unknown, though children need training to do this properly.

Journeys provide new experiences and inspire conversation. In this world of ours it is important that children should be able to express themselves by talking. Although at times 'silence is golden', the art of conversation has to be encouraged. This may be done through drama or through discussions in the classroom which are derived from some experience out of school. For those few children who are shy or timid certain opportunities have to be 'arranged' by the teacher. Perhaps children could look at each other's paintings and pass comments; a map of a journey might evoke reminiscences, or some of the slides and photographs will trigger off useful dialogue. But it would be a pity if the chance for conversation was missed after an exciting school journey. By talking about the day's happenings the children are reinforcing their knowledge by sharing it with each other.

**Worksheets**
Some teachers claim that every trip, if it is to be truly educational, must be accompanied by preparatory work and follow-up work. The 'hardliners' would also impose tasks to be done *en route*. But whatever the ideology, the worksheet is a useful device for directing work. The recently published book *Activity Methods in the Middle Years* (Greig and Brown 1975) devotes some space to workcard theory and is well worth perusal. But some general guidelines might, at this stage, prove useful. They are taken from examples of worksheets used by teachers on school and class trips.

Poorly produced worksheets are pretty useless. They do very little to inspire enthusiasm and if they can't be read or are full of errors they are a disgrace to the profession. By the use of heat copiers or electronic scanners, stencils can be made with diagrams and illustrations so that they are exactly right for the excursion in hand. They will be tailormade for a specific journey. Make a few extra copies to file away in the resources area: it will save time referring to them on a subsequent journey.

One tip from experience: if you are using Letraset or its equivalent to provide variety and quality in the lettering, then don't forget to spray the original before you feed into a heat copier. Otherwise it will almost completely disintegrate – ruining both original and stencil.

Card can be fed through most duplicators if you do it gently one at a time.

You might prefer to make your worksheets into a pleasant booklet, leaving spaces for answers and information which will be gleaned at a later stage by the tripper. In this case you might consider using only one side of the paper. Sometimes printing on both sides causes a headache for the teacher – especially if the duplicator is not working well.

## CONTENT

The worksheets will be made to suit the children – not *vice versa*. It may be necessary to modify the style and the content with differing ages and abilities. One worksheet supplied very kindly by Oxford County Museum Service at Woodstock contained a well-drawn picture and just one sentence which asked the children to write down what they had seen in a certain room. Another worksheet drew their attention to specific points in a display, leaving spaces for the missing items to be described by name. On a visit to a power station in Staffordshire some children were shown a film. There followed a questionnaire with thirteen specific questions based upon power stations, coal and electricity. Then followed three more pages of closely typed questions which made the discovery work seem very intense. A school trip to Chester was accompanied by a badly produced booklet to give the historical background to the ancient city. There were mistakes in the history, including the Roman name for Chester, and, as the spirit stencil was run off on to ordinary paper, the booklet was very difficult to read. Another school, however, had a trip to

Chester and produced an excellent booklet by use of electronic stencils and coloured inks. Its twenty-four pages included pictures, diagrams, maps, animal outlines, an itinerary and many different and interesting tasks to do. The workbook used by a group of children on a visit to Boscobel House had a varied content – things to look for *en route*, a history of the Civil War, and a detailed description of what to see and look for in a farm visit. The important thing to remember is that the worksheet or booklet is the main resource for the journey. It should reflect the interests and capabilities of the children on the trip.

QUESTIONS
Children like the challenge of answering questions. Try to follow one or two simple rules of thumb:

1  The children must understand the question.
2  The question should stand in its own right and not depend upon another correct answer before it makes sense.
3  Avoid too many Yes/No responses and give some open-ended questions which allow opinions and thought to flourish.
4  Don't kill enthusiasm by putting too many questions together: break up the working part of the text with illustrations so that it isn't too formidable.
5  Seek variety in the way you phrase the questions and give scope for spontaneous and original answers.
6  Remember the questions are not the be-all and end-all of the exercise. Give opportunities for sketching, note-taking and observations.

Variety is the spice of life so don't let your worksheets become as predictable in content and format as a reading laboratory. Try to preserve that valuable element of originality. Each trip will be different.

**Notebooks and diaries**
For those who don't like the restrictive and narrow approach of the questionnaire or worksheet a far better technique to use is the more open-ended keeping of a daily diary. This is, perhaps, more appropriate to a study week than a one-day journey. Each day the children can set aside some time to record the events of the day, the things which appealed to them, the things they didn't like and the comments they have to make. These books help in the

development of the critical faculty as the children state their preferences and refer to their likes and dislikes. They also have the advantage of flexibility of expression if the children are allowed to draw, to write, to calculate, to plot and to stick in items which appeal to their own particular interests.

Teresa, a girl of charm and liveliness, produced a diary with the following items:

1 The country walk
2 The old lady's visit
3 Headington
4 Our daily menus – and what I thought of them
5 Woodstock and the museum visit
6 Blenheim Palace and the trip on the lake
7 Our daily routine

It was illustrated with felt-tip drawings and gravestone rubbings and an occasional Polaroid photograph. Altogether it filled twenty pages of A4-size paper. Not a bad effort for four days' work, bearing in mind that each day was packed with activity.

Teachers using this approach must be prepared for surprises when they read what actually happened and what seemed so important to the children. It might give an insight into what children like. In this connection it is very interesting to note that Teresa makes no mention of the games and the evening treasure hunt. This was a highlight of some of the other accounts. If teachers want their journeys to be a success they should welcome this sort of feedback from the children.

It is significant that some of those children who spent a week in Oxford are still discussing it a year later. Who can claim that such ventures are not extremely worthwhile, in spite of the demands they make, both on staff and resources?

**A suggestion**
Keep a written record of the organizational details of your trip or journey. It may be very useful later on. Arrange suitable ways in which the children can gather their thoughts and share their experiences. Use variety in the approach so that follow-up work is not stereotyped or boring.

When some children from Lyndhurst returned from their Worcester trip, they decided for themselves how to present their own personal record. Some made up large charts with maps, pictures and written reminiscences: others made a little book, either in concertina or loose-leaf form. One boy, Dean Stevens, wrote the following account with great zest and enthusiasm:

On Tuesday, 15 June, we went to Worcester. The first thing we saw was the Tudor House. We went round the outside displays first and we saw carts which used to travel along Friar Street to get to the market. Then there was the Penny Farthing which was very common in the 1880s. It was very hard to ride. And there was a large black boiler with several others which had been used to keep Worcester Cathedral warm during the winter months. It was made by Gurney's Company. Then we went to the Town Tavern which was once an inn called the Cross Keys. There was a bowling alley at the rear. The last brewery to operate in Worcester was run by Speckley and Company. It closed down in 1968. There were four beer pumps in the tavern and a bench to sit on. Near the bench was a spitoon – a basin to use to stop the customers from spitting on the floor. Then we went to the record room where there were record players with spare needles and other things. Upstairs they had the Victorian Bedroom. The bed was bumpy and the blanket was made of knitted cotton. There were chairs in the room and one had a night shirt for men on it. The mattress was made of feather. In the Victorian times candles were the only light in the bedrooms. After that we went to the children's room. The earliest prams were the three wheelers which were very dangerous for fidgety children and so accidents happened quite often. The first four wheeled pram was not let onto the pavements for it had four wheels and was classed as a road vehicle. In Edwardian times black was considered to be the smartest colour for prams. Most of the schoolroom equipment came from St Paul's School Worcester which only closed down in 1970. After we had looked at everything else we went to the Cathedral.

The Cathedral had lots of seats and as soon as you went in you could hear the organ playing. The sound was creepy and scarey. It was the biggest place I have ever been in. The seats had carvings of kings and animals and carts. After I had seen King John's tomb I went down to the crypt. The walls were made of brick and it was very cold down there. When we came out of it, on top of the door above us, was a cross. It was about a foot long and a foot wide. Then I went to a souvenir shop and bought a pen. It had Worcester Cathedral on it.

So the writing continues. Dean gives many details of a trip which obviously gave him great enjoyment – even buying two bottles of 'Canada Dry' on the river boat which his friend paid for and which they consumed under the 'shelter thing'. Trips are worth while when they give the children so much to write and talk about.

**Reference**
GREIG, T. D. and BROWN, J. C. (1975) *Activity Methods in the Middle Years* Oliver and Boyd

Chapter 10

# Some golden rules

Experience, it is claimed, is the world's best teacher. The trouble
with that philosophy is that it implies that it takes a long time for
anyone to learn – and, presumably, they learn by their mistakes:
'You can't put an old head on young shoulders'. But teaching is
essentially the same as communicating, whatever the media, and
it is a process which thrives on the sharing of ideas. 'There's
nothing new' could quite well be the cry of the cynic, yet it is a fact
that in the teaching situation no two days are the same and the
rapport between teacher and pupil has a certain quality of
immediacy and a uniqueness. Whatever the teacher is doing, and
however he is doing it, it is always different; it is always fresh and
spontaneous. A good teacher never allows himself to be bored.
His problem is rather one of 'which of these things shall be our
priority for today?'. Even within the framework of a highly
structured scheme of work the originality which stems from
human interaction means that it is impossible to predict exactly
what will happen and what will result from the ideas and
transactions shared between the participants in the learning
process. So there has to be a compromise. The teacher sets out
with certain aims or objectives. He plans ways and means of
achieving these but, in the light of reality, some are attained more
easily than others. Some prove unsuitable in the light of changing
circumstances, so they are altered or dropped completely.
Flexibility becomes a part of the stock-in-trade of the wise teacher
for it is only by seizing the moment and doing the right thing that
he can survive. Children soon lose confidence in the teacher who
cannot make decisions, or procrastinates to hide his inefficiency.
Such behaviour is extravagant in the relative security of the
classroom: but on a journey or outing it can become devastating,
if not criminal.

So when offering 'golden rules' it is important to stress two things. The rules have derived from past experiences with children out of school and are not necessarily original or different: they are meant as a guide to sanity and satisfaction and are in no way intended as a panacea. Behind their humour and light-hearted presentation there is a serious concern. The author hopes that they will help the tripper to plan an outing with care; to consider how the children will be supervised and with what degree of freedom; and to ease the burden of responsibility so that the trip is enjoyable. Children can spot deceit and insincerity a mile off, so be honest, straightforward and firm, and they'll respect you for it!

### Don't put all your sandwiches in one rucksack
One teacher tells of his unfortunate experience in the Lake District. A party of intrepid walkers were crossing a mountain stream: half-way across the stepping stones one member fell in backwards. He was carrying the rucksack with all the food. Most of it was soaked and spoiled. If it had been shared out slightly better, then at least there would have been half a lunch. The same principle applies to money and valuables. Don't keep everything in the same container. If misfortune strikes then all is lost – a wise campaigner does not put all his eggs in the same basket.

### Count them every three minutes
Coach travel has its disadvantages, but it does provide a relatively easy form of supervision. Count the children frequently, especially on and off the coach, and don't let the driver pull away until everyone is on board. Be particularly careful when there are other school parties. On one occasion a school brought back an extra little girl with them from Twycross Zoo. She had joined the 'human snake', and got the wrong coach. What's more, she was too young, or too upset, to even realize until the coach had set off on the return journey. Imagine the consternation for the teachers who had lost her as well as those who found her sitting quietly on their coach. If there is adequate small grouping of children with a member of staff or parent, then this counting will be made far simpler. Children can go to their adult, who reports to the party leader. Don't be ashamed to call the register if it means trip efficiency. Do it at certain points along the way.

### Find those toilets
Children are very good at filling up with drinks, sweets, ices and

anything which is vaguely edible. But remember they need to 'lighten ship' also. Arrange stops along the route where this is possible. Instruct the young children to go to the toilet before they set out. Plan your excursion with toilet and victualling facilities very much in mind. Carry a spare toilet roll with you on country walks. It may prove to be worth its weight in gold. Remember cups of tea, Coca Cola, orange squash and soup are all good drinks – but that one extra drink might prove to be very expensive if the party misses its connection. Never take a large party to the Derby unless you arrange special toileting facilities! Mixed parties need mixed leaders for, even in the days of sexual equality, toilets remain a 'world apart'.

### Don't panic

Children need confidence. As the doctor said, if you appear to know what you are doing they will be impressed: if you panic and go to pieces so will they. If someone is missing think carefully before anyone else is despatched to find them, or you may lose yet another person. Arrange the timing of the trip with the age and inclination of the children in mind. If they become ego-involved then they will be reluctant to rush from one place to another. This factor should be borne in mind on zoo trips. Make sure that the children are in small groups; synchronize watches; arrange meeting places if you are going to split up; ensure first aid equipment is easy to get at; don't let the children get too near the animals. Is there something wrong? If so, be calm, count to ten, think of the other children and having decided on the necessary action, take it.

### Coach and train recognition

The pun is intended. When you get off a coach make sure the children know its number. The colour and make will not do. If the coach park fills up you may have a difficult job recognizing yours. Look for a means of locating the vehicle's position. Is it near a wall, a gateway, a fence? Which way did you turn when you came out of the car park? Some adults, as well as children, have very little sense of direction. Play games like 'I spy', and coach and train their recognition.

### Ban glass bottles, chocolate and pickled onions

Released from parental bondage and strengthened with packages of food, many children can't resist the urge to devour it all before the coach has disappeared out of the range of school. Take the initiative: ban eating on the coach; forbid the sight of bottles, chocolate or pickled onions. There will be less sickness, less litter, and both the children and the driver will benefit from the amnesty. If you are taking packed lunches – and costs of eating out make that virtually inevitable – then be sure that a site is arranged where they can be eaten. Try to ensure that this place is one which will afford shelter and protection from the worst that the British weather can devise. Nowadays canned drinks are all the rage. These can be a cause of sickness. Some children will have shandy or lager. See that these are drunk at the correct time and in the proper place. Don't let the children spoil the countryside, or the town for that matter, with their empty cans. It is wise to take a large polythene bag with you for keeping rubbish together. If necessary this can be brought back to the school dustbins!

## Watch out for traffic

No one likes accidents, and teachers have to pay particular attention to road safety when they are in charge of a group of children. There should be established procedures with regard to crossing the road and precautions should be taken when there is a chance that children will be out on their own. The problem is to be safe and secure without resorting to complete regimentation. When visiting foreign countries where the traffic is on the other side of the road, coping with the situation can be a traumatic experience. Make sure that no child is ever alone. They should be in small groups at least. Try and arrange that at least one is wearing a watch and that they know where to meet in case of emergency or difficulty. The age of the pupils does make a difference. Infants will need far more direct supervision than older children. In this respect holiday centres and traffic-free play areas have a distinct advantage when deciding upon the venue for a journey. Discipline is an attitude of mind fostered by respect, understanding and rapport between teachers and taught. It should be made very plain that when a group of teachers – possibly from different schools – are working together, then all the children and all the staff share the same bonds. Children should do as they are told when it is a matter of all-round safety. They should not be allowed to argue with 'Sir' or 'Miss' because it is not their regular teacher. Particular care should be exercised in getting on and off coaches, trains and boats. These moments are the dangerous ones when careless and daydreaming children are exposed to traffic risks. Teachers can help by strategically supervising the children: there should be someone at the beginning of a queue, someone near the middle and someone bringing up the rear. It sounds like common sense but it is vital.

## Be prepared

The Boy Scouts' motto has great relevance for teachers on school journeys. Before the trip starts, the teacher should go through it mentally and try to identify needs and possible dangers. First aid, food, exercise, rest and toilets are all basic essentials. Timetables, finances and contingency plans are also of paramount importance. Remember that those people who are not on the trip – parents and guardians and those still in school – need to know what is happening, so establish a communications network. Arrange to telephone the school or a chosen parent if there are delays or unavoidable changes, and try to prevent unneccesary worry by keeping people at home informed of what is going on. Have enough staff helpers to cover for moments when one teacher may have to do the unexpected and, in moments of stress, try to keep up that air of calmness – even if it is a facade.

## Join in the spirit

It's not a bit of good having miserable people on a school journey. Try to avoid taking the inefficient, grumpy teachers with you. The work is very hard and very tiring, but when it is all successfully over it gives a special glow of satisfaction, a sense of magnificent achievement. Look for lively colleagues who have a zest for life and a sense of adventure. There is always room for a sense of humour too. Teachers who are not prepared to make that extra effort which a trip or journey involves should be left back at school. They are a liability to the rest of the party and more trouble than all the children put together. When it comes to eating and sleeping in a foreign country, where there are different habits, one must join in the spirit and not expect everything to be just the same as it always is at home. Variety, after all, is an integral part of the experience and if it is buns and jam for breakfast instead of bacon and eggs then it is not much use wanting it to be otherwise. Those who enter into the spirit of the occasion gain the most from it.

## Work hard and play hard

This is an ideal philosophy for the teacher. If he is to remain on top of his job he needs to do both. Funnily enough, this attitude does rub off on the children. If they see that their teacher cares about standards and about doing things properly, they will be inclined to do the same. The sloppy teacher is hardly likely to impress children and, after a short time, they will lose respect for him through his inadequacies. Make it a rule that you are going to be industrious and efficient – even to the point of ruthlessness, but show them also that you know how to enjoy yourself when it comes to those precious moments of leisure. Work hard *and* play hard.

**Remember an army marches on its stomach**
Children need to eat. Plan your trips with this in mind. If there are to be country walks or rambles, then think about what will happen at lunchtime. Apart from the food, think about the shelter. One boy passed out on a hot summer day and had to go to hospital – he had a low blood sugar and the combination of the coach ride, the heat and the lack of a good breakfast nearly caused disaster. It also ruined the trip as everyone was concerned for his well-being and worried as to his state of health. Have a good meal in the morning, a snack at lunchtime and something substantial in the evening. Avoid swigging cans of fizzy pop and eating green ice-lollies *en route* and if you are abroad forbid the drinking of unbottled water. A dose of the dreaded lurgi can ruin any trip completely. Don't allow children to go without food just because it's not the same as at home.

**Keep a list handy**
One of the most useful items one can have near at hand in an emergency is a comprehensive list of the children's names, addresses and telephone numbers. It saves time and embarrassment in trying to communicate with others and it serves many purposes. Don't be ashamed to 'call the register' if you are checking on your group – the list will serve that purpose very well and it will save time if you want to ascertain a child's home telephone number. If he or she is ill or lost they may be unable to tell you for themselves. Each teacher should have a copy of these basic facts, so why not duplicate the list? Use a stencil and roll off sufficient copies for everyone concerned. It is better than having to recopy names again and again!

**If you don't love them, don't take them out**
A final word to school trippers. If you don't want the bother of

looking after children for the whole duration of the trip or journey and if you aren't able to share their enthusiasm for the mundane, then avoid any sort of school trip as you would avoid the plague.

Trips of every sort demand a great deal of the staff. They cause headaches, both real and imagined. They demand a great deal of energy and zest. At times, the pressures seem to be out of all proportion to the results. But, on the other hand, these excursions bring a new perspective to the child's awareness of life and their value, though immeasurable, is very significant, in terms of knowledge and experience gained.

A good trip is like a good meal. It has to be carefully prepared, properly savoured, balanced with sweet and sour, mixed with substance and garnished with little extras to make it attractive and tempting and then digested. If the ingredients are poor, then the results will be mediocre – even off-putting. In order to enjoy a trip, the teacher and his pupils must work at it together. It is far harder than merely sitting in the comparative safety and security of the classroom. If the teacher can't be bothered with trivia and is devoid of love and understanding for his children, then he's probably a very poor teacher, but he will certainly be hopeless when it comes to running a successful trip, and he would be well advised to find some means of getting out of doing it!

A cynic, who knows the cost of everything and the value of nothing, would say that school journeys are to be avoided: in contrast, a dedicated teacher sees them as an ideal opportunity for fun, fellowship and learning and a broadening of social experience.

Good luck to you all when you set off on your next adventure!

Appendix 1

# Sample explanatory letter to parents

**Lyndhurst Primary School**

3rd May 1976

*Educational Visit to Drayton Manor Park*
*Wednesday 26th May 1976*

Dear Parent,
We are taking the children from Class 6 to Drayton Manor Park
this year. Mothers, fathers and friends are welcome. The cost will
be 85p each which will cover coach fare and entrance fee to the
Park.
 A packed lunch and a 'mack' will be needed. The coach will
leave school at 9.15 am and will return at 3.30 pm approximately.
 If you would like your child to go on this outing, please fill in
the attached slip and return it to school as soon as possible.

Yours sincerely
*G. Tait*

---

**Form of consent**

I                                          the parent or guardian
of                                         consent to my child taking
part in the visit to Drayton Manor Park on Wednesday the 26th
May 1976 in accordance with the arrangements which have been
explained to me. I agree that such alterations may be made in
them as circumstances necessitate.

Signed                              Date

# Sample parents' and medical consent forms from an education committee

## CITY OF BIRMINGHAM EDUCATION COMMITTEE

**Stansfeld Country Study Centre**

**Parents' Consent Form**

*Name of pupil* (block capitals)
*Address* (block capitals)

*Date of birth*                              *School*

I                the father/mother/guardian of
consent to my son/daughter taking part in a visit to Stansfeld
Country Study Centre in accordance with arrangements which
have been explained to me. I agree that such alterations may be
made in them as the circumstances necessitate.

I understand that while the school staff-in-charge of the party
will take all reasonable care of the pupils, they cannot necessarily
be held responsible for any loss, damage or injury suffered by my
son/daughter arising during or out of the school journey.

Signed                              Date

*The form on the reverse of this Parents' Consent Form must also be
completed.*

P.T.O.

# CITY OF BIRMINGHAM EDUCATION COMMITTEE

**Stansfeld Country Study Centre**

**Medical Consent Form**

*Name of pupil* (block capitals)
*Address* (block capitals)

*Telephone number*
or *Telephone number of neighbour in case of emergency*

*Religion*                                    *Date of birth*

*Confidential*
When did your son/daughter last receive a Tetanus Injection?
Does your son/daughter suffer from any of the following ailments?

## ASTHMA  HAYFEVER  ALLERGIES  FITS  DIABETES

If so, please state ailment and medication used

Please give below information about any illness and medical treatment which your son/daughter is currently receiving or has received during the last month

I being the father/mother/guardian of                    declare that he/she has not received any form of medical treatment during the past month nor is he/she under any medical investigation at the present time.

*Signed*                                    *Dated*

I agree to my child receiving any emergency treatment, dental, medical or surgical (including the administration of anaesthetics) that may be advised by the doctor during my child's stay at Stansfeld Country Study Centre.

*Signed*                                    *Dated*
*Pupil's Doctor's name and address*

*Pupil's National Health number*
*School*

# Sample school visit forms from Nansen Primary School

**School Visit Costing Details**        Nansen J.I. School

*Educational Visit*

Visit to                   Date

Number of children on visit with parents' permission

Any amendment to previous proposal, i.e. change of leaders etc.

Transport arrangements i.e. no. of coach/es, name of firm

*Costs*   Transport
        Insurance charges
        Admittance charges
        Meals or drinks
        Any other costs

Cost per child

Names of any children who should receive financial assistance. These children *should not* be notified of any concession at this stage.

Signed                       Date

---

*Office Section*

Above visit and details approved with teacher in charge

Issued to teacher in charge:
    Collecting cards for children
    Collecting sheets for teachers
    Balance sheet

**School Visit Proposal Form**                    Nansen J.I. School

*Educational Visit or School Journey*

Proposed visit
Date                                    Times
Classification of visit      A1      A2      A3      A4
Delete appropriately       B1      B2      B3      C1      C2
Class/es participating
Teacher in charge
Other party leaders (teachers)


Other adult escorts


Signed                                    Date

---

*Office Section*
Above visit approved with teacher in charge
East District Managers informed if other than A1 or A2
Issued to teacher in charge:
   Insurance form
   Parent consent forms
   Costing sheet


**Pupil's details sheet**

| Personal Information to be carried with you on the visit | NANSEN PRIMARY SCHOOL |
|---|---|
| Name | VISITS COLLECTION CARD |
| Address | Name<br>Class |
| In case of accident please inform | Visit to |
| | Date |
| Phone No. | Cost |

145

K

**Payments**

| Date | Amount paid | Amount owing | Signature |
| --- | --- | --- | --- |
| | | | |

*Points to remember*

1  Be punctual – leave home early enough or you may be left behind.
2  Do not stray away from your group.
3  Do not leave your seat in the coach without permission.
4  Look after your spending money very carefully. (Mend the holes in your pockets.) Put name and address inside your purse.
5  No bottles or tins of drinks of any kind are to be brought. If you want an extra drink use a plastic container or plastic bottle.
6  Wear sensible shoes.
7  Bring a raincoat with you. Make sure it is marked with your name.
8  Do not bring a radio.
9  Do not drop litter in the coach or elsewhere. If there is not a waste bin then bring your rubbish with you until one is found.
10  Behave yourself properly. Your school will be judged on your behaviour.

*Have a good time.*

Reminders for this trip

# Example of a worksheet from the Museum of Oxford

### Potteries by the Roman Road

The Romans did not build a town at Oxford, but there was one at Dorchester, just 10 miles away. The road from there to another Roman town – Alchester – passed close to where Headington is now. Near the road were the homes and workshops of native Britons who made pots and sold them to the Romans, and to those Britons who had adopted a Roman way of life. This worksheet is about those pottery workshops especially the ones which were found by archaeologists in the grounds of the Churchill Hospital, where this kiln comes from. It was being used by potters to fire pots in about 350 AD.

In the display case you will find two sorts of pottery; bowls for preparing food (mortaria) and others for serving it in. They are different from the sort of pots the native Britons had made before the Romans came to Britain.

The area we call Headington was a good place for making pottery. There were trees and bushes all around for fuel, and it was easy to dig sand, grit and clay from sloping ground nearby. The Roman road was not far off, so when the bowls were finished they could be loaded on to packhorses and carried off down the road, or down to the barges waiting on the river.

At first the pots were sold to Romans who lived nearby or in local towns but by 300 AD people in faraway parts of southern England were using Oxford pottery. Perhaps some enterprising villa owner bought all the pottery and made a big profit by selling it in other parts of the country.

1   *The Roman road*
On the map find the road that leads from Dorchester. Where does it go?

Find the place on the map where the kiln was found. Is it far from the Roman road?

The finished pots were carried by packhorses through the woods and along the road. They could also be transported by water. What river do you think they would have travelled on?

2   *The sort of pots they made*
These bowls were used for grinding food and mixing it up. What is their proper name?

Something has been left out in the picture. Draw in the missing part.
The bottom of the bowls were rough to make it easier to grind things. What makes them rough?

Find this bowl in the display case. It is made of a light coloured clay which archaeologists call 'Parchment ware'. Bowls like this were used at the table. On the picture draw in pencil the decoration you would use if you were a Romano-British potter. What colour would you use?

Find this pot in the display case.
(a)   What do you think it was used for?

(b)   What is it called?

All these pots were made on a wheel. Look at the picture on the front of this worksheet; it shows what the wheel probably looked like. How did the potter make the wheel go round?

How are potter's wheels turned today?

Sometimes the potter scratched or stamped his name on a pot. Find out the name of one who did this. Write it here:

3  *How the kiln worked*
When the potter had made the pots on his wheel they were soft and damp. They had to be carefully dried out and then baked in a kiln to make them hard and strong.

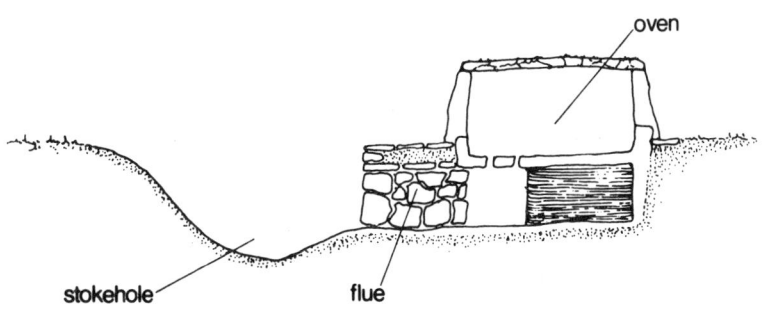

oven

stokehole          flue

In this picture the kiln has been cut in half to show you how it worked. The potter stood in the stokehole and made the fire in the flue. The heat went into the oven and heated the pots which were stacked on top of each other on the floor. Draw the potter, the fire, and the pots in the right places. Did the potter put the pots in through the flue or through the top? (The picture on the front of this worksheet will help you.)

Look at the kiln. It was dug out of sandy ground. What was the inside made of?

Part of the kiln is missing now. Which part?

Would it work without that part?

There is a big hole in the floor which would not have been there. The small holes would have been there. What for?

This kiln was in use in about 370 AD. How old is it now?

Draw the potter (a stick-man will do) to complete the pictures.

| 1 | 2 | 3 |
|---|---|---|
| First the potter dug the clay. | He turned it on a wheel. | When the bowls had dried out he put them in a kiln. |
| 4 | 5 | 6 |
| Then he stoked the fire. | He sold his pots to Romans. | He loaded some pots onto packhorses. |

Now you have found out something about the potteries by the Roman road here are some ideas for other things to do either at school or at home.

*Make a pot*
The mortaria were designed especially for grinding and mixing food. Can you design a bowl for a special purpose – for example carrying water? Make a bowl of your own design in clay or in Plasticine.

See if you can make a pot like one of those on display, and decorate it to look the same.

*Paint*
Try painting the scene at the Headington workshop on a busy day, with the potters at their wheels, and the kiln in use.

*Make a frieze*
You could use the same idea to make a frieze to go around the wall of your room. Perhaps some friends would help; you could each do a different thing – a potter, a kiln, a packhorse, some mortaria etc. and then stick the finished pieces onto a long piece of paper.

*Write a story*
Imagine you are a potter, or a villa owner and describe what goes on at the Headington pottery workshop.

*Find out*
Find out how the Romans lived and what they ate. (Some of the books on the list will help.) Here is a recipe from one of the books to whet your appetite!

Turnover as a sweet:
Toast pine-kernels and broken and clean nuts, and pound with honey, pepper, liquamen, milk, eggs, a little wine and oil. Cook in a shallow pan and turn out on to a round serving dish.
(from *Apicius: The Roman Cookery Book*)

*Places to visit*
Unfortunately you cannot see anything at the Churchill Hospital

site, but you can visit the Ashmolean Museum in Beaumont Street to find out more about the Romans. You could also go and see the remains of the Roman villa at North Leigh.

*Here are some books to read*
(The ones with a * beside them are for older readers)
*\*Apicius: The Roman Cookery Book* edited by B. Flower and E. Rosenbaum, published by Harrap
*\*Britain in the Roman Empire* Joan Liversidge, published by Routledge and Kegan Paul
*Your Book of Roman Britain* David Jones, published by Faber
*Invaded Island – A Pictorial History – The Stone Age to 1086* R. J. Unstead, published by Macdonald

# Bibliography

ADAMS, A. (1976) *The Humanities Jungle* Ward Lock Educational
BARRELL, G. R. (1975) *Teachers and the Law* Methuen
BARRY, C. H. and TYE, F. (1972) *Running a School* Temple Smith
BATEMAN, R. (1971) *Leisure in the Seventies* Stanley Paul
BOURNE, R. and MACARTHUR, B. (1970) *The Struggle for Education* Schoolmaster Publishing Company
BROWNRIGG, R. (1968) *Come and See* Darton, Longman and Todd
COWIE, D. (1972) *Switzerland: The Land and the People* Yoseloff
DES (1967) *Children and their Primary Schools* (Plowden Report) HMSO
EDWARDS, T. (1950) *The Face of Wales* Batsford
GREIG, T. D. and BROWN, J. C. (1975) *Activity Methods in the Middle Years* Oliver and Boyd
HADFIELD, C. and STREAT, M. (1971) *Holiday Cruising on Inland Waterways* David and Charles
HAIGH, G. (1974) *Out of School Activities* Pitman
HARE, R. (1970) *Know How: A Student Guide to Project Work* Intertext Books
HARRISON, M. (1970) *Learning Out of School* Ward Lock Educational
HASSETT, J. and WEISBERG, A. (1972) *Open Education* Prentice-Hall
HEMERY, E. (1970) *Wilderness Camping in Britain* Robert Hale
HOGAN, J. M. (1970) *Beyond the Classroom* Educational Explorers
HUNT, N. (1969) *Camping* (Illustrated Teach Yourself Series) Brockhampton Press
KENT, G. (1970) *Teaching After School* Ward Lock Educational

MCLEAN, D. (ed) (1970) *It's People That Matter* Angus and Robertson

MERRITT, J. (1974) *What Shall We Teach?* Ward Lock Educational

MIDWINTER, E. (1975) 'Curriculum and the EPA school' in Golby, Greenwald and West *Curriculum Design* Open University

NELSON, N. (1975) *Belgium and Luxembourg* Batsford

OLLIS, M. (1973) *Boarders Away* Longman

PLUCKROSE, H. (1975) *Open School, Open Society* Evans Brothers

POLLARD, M. (1976) *A Handbook of Resources for Primary Schools* Ward Lock Educational

SCHOOLS COUNCIL (1972) *British Primary Schools Today* Macmillan Education

SCHOOLS COUNCIL (1975) *School Outdoor Resource Areas* (from Project Environment 8–18) Longman

SCHWEBEL, M. and RAPH, J. (1973) *Piaget in the Classroom* Routledge and Kegan Paul

# Index